Stonehenge Antiquaries

Stonehenge Antiquaries

by Rodney Legg

*Published by the Dorset Publishing Company,
Knock-na-cre, Milborne Port, Sherborne,
Dorset DT9 5HJ*

Publishing details. First published in 1986.
Copyright extends to modern text © Rodney
Legg 1986, and also subsists in the presentation
and layouts © Dorset Publishing Company
1986. Robert Gay's *A Fool's Bolt* was previously
published in 1725, and J. Easton's *Conjectures* in
1815. The Thomas Hardy article *Shall Stonehenge
Go* appeared in 1899. The second edition of Lord
Eversley's *Commons, Forests and Footpaths* was
published in 1910. All authors, with the exception
of Rodney Legg, are out of copyright and are
reproduced here as a compilation of source
material from which scholars may quote freely in
the future. Jacob Simon's letter to *The Times*
is reproduced with the writer's kind permission.

International Standard Book Number 0 902129 32 5

Printing details. Main modern typesetting by
Photosetting and Secretarial Services, Station
Approach, Yeovil, with layouts by Tony Pritchard.
Printed by Creed Printers at
Broadoak, near Bridport, Dorset, with platemaking
by Linda Dare.

1.
A Fool's Bolt soon shott at Stonage

by Robert Gay

First published, anonymously in *Peter Langtoft's Chronicle* in 1725

Introduction

by Rodney Legg, the annotator of the
First Edition of John Aubrey's
Monumenta Britannica

THE PRIMARY clue to the authorship of *A Fool's Bolt* is a
note from Rev. Andrew Paschall, the rector of Chedzoy
near Bridgwater at the time of the Monmouth rebellion
and the writer of the most detailed account that survives
of the Battle of Sedgemoor. He was later a member of the
bishop's staff at Wells. Information from Paschall is
quoted by John Aubrey, the antiquary, in his
Monumenta Britannica (Volume One, first printed 1980
by Dorset Publishing Company):

"*Mr. Paschall's letter – The author of the 'Bolt soon Shot', was
one of Mr .... Jay of Nettlecombe lying in the western parts of
Somersetshire, deceased (I think) 14, or 16 years since.*
Yours &c. A. P.   *Wells, April 7. 1690.*"

Nettlecombe is in the foothills of Exmoor, to the south of Williton. Nettlecombe Court, an extensive country house, stands beside the church and was the home of the Trevelyan family in the 17th century. It remained in their hands for a further three centuries. The buildings are now the Leonard Wills Centre of the Field Studies Council, and 21,000 people have attended courses there in its first decade. The parish owns the earliest known hallmarked plate in existence, a pre-reformation chalice and paten dated between 1439 and 1479, though these are usually kept at the Victoria and Albert Museum.

J. H. Crothers, the warden at the centre, is the editor of the journal *Field Studies.* He provided a copy for 1970 (Vol. 3, No. 2), which has a paper on Nettlecombe Court by R. J. E. Bush. In it is a note that an "assault had been made on the house in 1643 by Robert Gay, the rector of Nettlecombe and a staunch parliamentarian, with a mob of similar sympathisers. They fired the outbuildings and made unsuccessful attempts to destroy Nettlecombe Court itself. As a result Gay was imprisoned but subsequently released, continuing as rector until his death in December 1672."

The search for the author of the *Fool's Bolt* seemed to be over. A note of caution was raised, however, by John Fowles. He has edited the first printing of *Monumenta Britannica,* and called at Nettlecombe Court to review the evidence:

"Jay and Gay could well be one and the same — the bird 'jay' was often written 'gay' 'geay' etc. in the 17th century Uplyme accounts I transcribed last year (1979) but I'm a bit puzzled why Andrew Paschall should have spelt it Jay. One might expect the spelling Gay or Geay if the name was pronounced Jay, but not vice versa.

"It also seems a little unusual that your Robert Gay should be presumably a devoted Puritan rector during the Commonwealth and still in office after the Restoration; perhaps he played his cards right, though. John Gay the poet, *Beggar's Opera,* etc, was born at Barnstaple, 1685, 'of ancient but impoverished Devonshire family' — so the name is 'local'. But if our Jay = Rev. Robert Gay, Paschall would have mentioned he was clergy?"

R. J. E. Bush, assistant county archivist at Somerset Record Office, and the writer of the Nettlecombe Court paper, expanded on his knowledge of Gay:

"I think there can be little doubt that the author of the work you mention was the Rev. Robert Gay, rector of Nettlecombe 1631-72. There is no family called Jay mentioned in the parish registers at the approximate date and Gay would have been one of the few literate inhabitants of that thinly populated rural parish.

"Robert Gay mentioned as a 'plebeian' from Somerset at Magdalen Hall, Oxford, òn 16 November 1621, aged 19. He graduated B.A. 21 October 1624 and M.A. on 1 June 1627 and subsequently, in 1629, incorporated at Cambridge (Foster, *Alumni Oxonienses).* Unfortunately the diocesan consignation books, which might have hinted at his origins, are blank where details of ordinations are generally given. He may have been the Robert Gay who signs the Chelwood bishop's transcript as curate in 1630. He was instituted rector of Nettlecombe on 22 April 1631 and by his wife, Martha (whom he did *not* marry at Nettlecombe) had the following children baptised: George on 8 December 1633, Robert on 5 July 1635, Elizabeth on 8 December 1636, Margaret on 1 November 1638, Martha on 18 December 1640, Frances on 7 November 1641, Nathaniel on 5 December 1642, Mary on 10 February 1654. There is a gap in the registers 1644-53 which may conceal the births of other children.

"Robert's wife Martha was buried on 2 March 1654 (probably as a result of a difficult childbirth), and he was buried on 18 December 1672. For the last two years of his incumbency he made no entries in the register. He thus earned the censure of his successor, Rev. William Griffin, who wrote in the register of Gay: 'that in his tyme there was a very great failure in registering the baptisms and burials of severall persons.'

"Nettlecombe is dominated by Nettlecombe Court, for centuries the home of the Trevelyan family. According to notes among the Trevelyan family papers, during the Civil War in 1643 Gay at the head of a mob attacked Nettlecombe Court, fired the outbuildings and made unsuccessful attempts to destroy the house. A letter of 28 August 1643 from Sir John Stawell to George Trevelyan indicated that Gay had been caught and imprisoned and was asking for a hearing concerning the complaints against him made to the Marquis of Hertford. An order also survives from Charles I at Oxford to Edmund Wyndham, Sheriff of Somerset, dated 11 October 1643, requiring that Gay 'having been lately imprisoned for being actually in rebellion against us', released on bail and re-arrested, that he might again be let out on bail so that he might attend his hearing.

"Robert Gay's imprisonment apparently led to Nettlecombe parish being served by Peter King, clerk, who occurs as occupying the Parsonage in poor rates of 1644 and 1645. No rate account survives for 1646 and by 1647 Gay was again in residence."

Gay's dates tie in well with the evidence that the *Fool's Bolt* provides. Its author refers to Inigo Jones's *Stonehenge Restored,* which was published in 1655. *Peter Langtoft's Chronicle,* in which the *Fool's Bolt* was first printed (in 1725) has a margin note about the manuscript being "lent me by James West, of Balliol College" (1722) and that it is "written in the same hand, and by the same anonymous author" as the previous paper in the same work. This is entitled: *A Discourse about some Roman Antiquities Discover'd near Conquest in Somersetshire, supposed to be the Place where the Romans Conquest of Britain was completed.* It begins with the author's report on the discovery "In that most critical year of our Lord 1666" of two hoards of Roman coins, at Lydeard St Lawrence and Stogumber. The *Fool's Bolt* is also likely to have been written in the 1660s.

The Conquest discourse is a fanciful catalogue of etymological misassumptions, though to put together such a list of minor placenames would have required a detailed knowledge of the Somerset levels and coastline. Many of the hamlets and hills that he mentions are not shown on 17th century maps. It is strong circumstantial evidence that the *Fool's Bolt* can be ascribed to someone from Somerset. The probability is that the author was Robert Gay.

Interest in the *Fool's Bolt* has been stimulated by John Fowles, who uses extracts from this work in his 1980 publication *The Enigma of Stonehenge* (Jonathan Cape). He points out that Gay's approach just about sums up the collective thoughts of all subsequent writers on the monument. Since "pedlars and tinkers, vamping on London way near it, may, and do, freely spend their mouthes on it," Gay sees no reason why he should not also "shoot his bolt" on the matter.

Fowles continues: "There is nothing else in all the enormous Stonehenge literature that can compare with this rancorous and sarcastic start to a *A Fool's Bolt*. A little later, just in case any reader might think they were dealing with a mere wit, not a scholar, Gay flashes out a long list of early English historians, from Gildas and Bede on, and points out that they were all silent before Stonehenge.

" 'This Stonage did astonish them, and did amaze them, that they durst not labour, lest they should lose their labour, and themselves also. And if the grand Seniors, which lived so near it, above a thousand years since, could not, how shall we sillie freshmen unlock this Closet?' He then (falling through those ever-luring stone 'doors') announces that he has 'stumbled on 2 picklocks, which, if dexterously handled, will set it wide open to the world.'

"They do not, of course; but the author is adamant that Stonehenge is an ancient British monument. The worthy Inigo Jones is curtly dismissed as 'Out-I-goe' Jones. Gay points out the very name is British - '*Stone hanging place,* because some remaines of it are like gallowes.' Etymology is indeed his forte, and in places it is carried to such hair-raising lengths that one half suspects that the whole essay (like his companion piece, *Claudius Caesar's Treasure)* is a seventeenth-century spoof — a dazzlingly prolonged mockery of scholarship that takes itself too seriously. But some of his ideas are shrewd, and plainly influenced Aubrey. Gay guessed that Stonehenge belonged to an original native population, before the Belgae, the Iron Age Celts from across the Channel; he concedes the Romans might have helped build it, but points out that the Greeks had contacts with ancient Britain long before Julius Caesar's time. Unfortunately he then plumps for a race of Somerset giants as builders, and cites evidence of their remains (which we can see were in fact animal fossils — one found very near Stonehenge was nearly fourteen feet long, with a tooth 'the quantity of a great wallnut').

"Nothing in this bizarre piece is more striking than the domination of word over fact, of book-learned conjecture over observation. It must remain the favourite text of all amateur fools, like myself, who shoot bolts at Stonehenge."

Opposite: *page of the Nettlecombe parish register, probably in Robert Gay's hand. Courtesy Somerset Record Office*

1660   Joane Kelley wid. was buried Aprill the 5th day

Joan: Gully the wife of George Gully was
buried the 20th day of May 1660
John Lawrence was buried the 17th day of June 1660
Simon Musgrave ... was buried ... the ...
Alice Woolcott the wife of John ...Woolcott
the elder was buried ... Sept 29th 1660
Christian Winter the daughter of John ...
and Joane his wife was buried ... 25th ...

1661   Elizabeth Bray the daughter of Robert Bray
and Elizabeth his wife was buried Apr 6: 1661
Elizabeth Swetman Widdowe was buried
June 25th 1661
John Winter was buried July 8th 1661
Marie Slade the wife of John Slade was buried
September 8 1661
Honnor Gunningham the wife of Mr William
Gunningham was buried September 6th 1661
Katherine Winter the daughter of Markt
Winter and Phillip his wife was buried
December ... 1661

1662   William How of St Drunmans was buried
Aprill 22th 1662
John Lane the sonne of John Lane and Marie
his wife was buried May 18th 1662
Margaret Gole the daughter of Maurice Gole
and Joane his wife was buried August 24: 1662
Johane Winter Widdow was buried
October ... 1662

1663   William Medford was buried March 1th 1663
Robert Fry was buried May 7
Mr B. Beard...ins ... was buried N... ...
Thomas Beddle was buried Aug 25 1663
John Woolcott the elder was buried Nov 9th 1663

1664   Jane Goodenow was buried Apr 16th
Margetts daughter of John Gunn was buried
May 31
Sibill Wari was buried Aug 2
Constance Woolcott was buried Octob 2

A Fool's Bolt soon shott at Stonage

A

DISCOURSE

CONCERNING

STONE-HENGE.

.ᴇ4

A

FOOL'S BOLT

SOON SHOTT AT

STONAGE.

From another MS. lent me by the same Friend, Mr. JAMES WEST, of BALLIOL-Coll. written in the same hand, and by the same anonymous Author.

WANDER witt of Wiltshire, rambling to Rome to gaze at Antiquities, and there skrewing himself into the company of Antiquaries, they entreated him to illustrate unto them, that famous Monument in his Country, called Stonage. His Answer was, that he had never seen, scarce ever heard of, it. Whereupon, they kicked him out of doors, and bad him goe home, and see Stonage; and I wish all such Æsopicall Cocks, as slight these admired Stones, and other our domestick [1] Monuments (by

---

[1] So called à monendo. Goldm. Dic.

which

which they might be admonished, to eschew some **evil,**
or doe some good) and scrape for barley Cornes of vanity out of forreigne dunghills, might be handled, or rather footed, as he was. If I had been in his place, I
should have been apt to have told them, that, surely, it
was some heathonish temple demolished by the immediate hand of God, as an intollerable abomination unto
him : yet reserving so much of it standing, as may declare what the whole was, and how, and why, so destroyed, that, as we are to remember Lot's wife, turned
into a Piller of Salt, for looking back-ward towards Idolatrous Sodome, so we should remember, that these for-
lorne Pillers of Stone are left to be our remembrancers,
dissuading us from looking back in our hearts upon any
thing of Idolatry, and persuading us, in imitation of
Moses, and the Prophets, so to describe, and deride, it in
it's uglie Coullers, that none of us, or our posterity, may
returne, with Doggs, to such Vomit, or Sows to wallow-
ing in such mire. And since all, that have (as yet) written on this Subject, have contradicted and confuted each
other, and never any hath as yet revealed this mysterie
of iniquity to this purpose, and that Pedlers and Tinckers,
vamping on London way near it, may, and do, freely
spend their mouthes on it, I know nothing to the contrary, but that I also may shoot my bolt a little farther into
it, however I will adventure, were it for nothing elce,
but to recreate my self somtimes, after other studies,
and to provoke my friends, which importun'd me to it,
to shoote their acute shafts at it also, hoping, that one
or other of us, by art or accident, shall hit the mark. My
bolt is soon shott in this short conjecture, that 𝖲𝗍𝗈𝗇𝖺𝗀𝖾
was an old British triumphall tropicall temple, erected to
Anaraith, their Godess of victory, in a bloudy field there,
wone,

wone, by illustrious *Stanengs* and his *Cangick Giants,* from K. *Diviliacus* and his *Belgæ.* In which temple the Captives and spoiles were sacrifised to the said Idol *Anaraith.* So that these 12 particulers hereof are to be demonstrated,

1. That Stonage was an old British Monument.
2. That it was a Monument of a bloody battel foughten there.
3. This bloudy battel produced a glourious Victorie.
4. This Victorie was wonne by the *Cangi* of Glad-erbaf.
5. The *Cangi* were Giants.
6. Commanded by the famous *Stanenges* of Honni-cutt.
7. The Army conquered, was K. *Divitiacus* and his *Belgæ.*
8. In this place, assoone as the *Cangi* had conquered, they triumphed.
9. Where they triumphed they erected this Monument as a Trophie.
10. This Trophie was a Temple.
11. This Temple was consecrated to *Anaraith,* their Goddess of Victorie.
12. In this temple the said Victors sacrifised their Captives and Spoiles to their said Idoll of Victorie.

Our work lies before us in these 12 particulers, and our tooles, to perform it, should be antcient and credible histories, treating of this subject. but what are they, and where to be found? Jeffrie of Monmouth will tell you a tale, that these Stones were brought by Giants
from

from Africa into 𝕼𝖚𝖎𝖑𝖉𝖆𝖗𝖊 in Ireland, and, by some Le-
gerdemaine of Merlin, conveyed to the place, where
they are; but no credible Historian could speke any
word of any such thing. *Gildas Badonicus* of Bathe,
within 20 Miles of 𝕾𝖙𝖔𝖓𝖆𝖌𝖊, writing *anno Domini* 543.
hath not a word of it, nor venerable *Bede*, who writing
anno 727. of many other rarities of this Land, hath not
a word of 𝕾𝖙𝖔𝖓𝖆𝖌𝖊, nor *William of Malms-burie*, writing *anno* 1142. within 14 miles of 𝕾𝖙𝖔𝖓𝖆𝖌𝖊, hath not
a word of it, nor *Ethelwred*, nor *Hoveden*, nor [1] *Ingul-
thus*, nor *Paris*, nor *Westmonasteriensis*, nor *Florentius
Wigorniensis*, who all wrote above 500 years since, yet
not a word of it; and *Henricus Huntingdoniensis*, writing near the same time, tells the naked truth of the Matter, that it was not because they would not, but because
they could not, say any thing of it. His words are [2]:
Quatuor sunt in Anglia, quæ mira videntur, scilicet 𝕾𝖙𝖆=
𝖓𝖊𝖓𝖌𝖊𝖘, *(i. e.)* 𝕾𝖙𝖔𝖓𝖆𝖌𝖊, *ubi lapides miræ magnitudinis
in modum portarum elevati sunt, ita ut portæ portis su-
perpositæ videantur, nec potest quis excogitare, quâ arte
tanti lapides adeo in altum elevati sunt, vel quare ibidem
constructi sunt.* This 𝕾𝖙𝖔𝖓𝖆𝖌𝖊 did astonish them, this
did amaze them, that they durst not labour, lest they
should [3] lost their labour, and themselves also. And if
the grand Seniors, which lived so near it, above a thousand years since, could not, how shall we sillie freshmen unlock this Closet? I have stumbled on 2 picklocks, which, if dexterously handled, will set it wide open
to the world.

1. A description of the fabrick of 𝕾𝖙𝖔𝖓𝖆𝖌𝖊, at least
of some part of it, as it was in it's primitive perfection.

---

[1] Pro, *Ingulfus.* H.   [2] Henric. Hunt. lib. 1°. Histo.   [3] F.
lose, vel *have lost.* H.

2. A

2. A mappe of Wiltshire.

1. As for a description of the saide fabricke, I would referr you to Architector Inigo Jones in his book, entituled, *Stonehenge restored*, but that some would be ready to say, the multitude of his Græcian Architectonicall termes of the parts of it, as *hypæthros, monopteros,* [1] *dipteros, architrave,* [2] *Pycnostylos, Scheame, peripteros, hexagon,* &c. do rather obscure then illustrate the same, and that, whereas he hath 10 designs of this fabrick all in folio, one in 4to. may serve the turn as well. Nay one whole one is to much; because the externall circle of high Stones will overshadow allmost all within them, as a company of tall men, standing round about a company of Children. And I think three or four Stones of each of the 5 Circles, with verball apprehensions of the number and dimension of the Stones of each circle, will give best intelligence to common capacities, which I endeavour to informe, and this I have done in the frontispice, and have added Characteristicall letters to each remarkable part and place of the fabrick, correlateing to what I shall say concerning such particulers.

2. The second pick-lock, to help the former, is a Mapp of Wiltshire, at least of the Hill Country about 𝕾tonage, describing the antient British Names of circumjacent Hills, Hamletts, Rivers, &c. For I conceive, that the old Britons, which lived in those places, took it for a great honour, that thence pittifull habitations should be called after the name of this antient renowned mount, or some part or propertie thereof, and this is most observable in those 3 eminent Rivers, 𝕮ellínburn, 𝖆von and 𝔐adder, runing from their severall quarters

---

[1] *Diptoros* MS. H. [2]*Pymostolos. Sheune. perupteros,* MS. *II.*

al-

almost to 𝔖tonage, and meeting a little below it, and in many of the hamletts, situate on, or near, those Rivers, up to their Fountaines, both the said Rivers, and many Villages on them, taking their antient British names, some from 𝔖tonage, some from some, some from other, parts and properties thereof, shortly after it was founded, and seeing, that *conveniunt rebus nomina,* and that any one of those antient names, taken from 𝔖ton‹ age, is a Description of the same, then, surely, out of many of those names, methodically composed, may a definition of it be formed, at least some such conjecture of mine aforesaid. And because this nominall picklock is of my invention, as he that forgeth a pick-locke will try him upon some doore of his own, before he will adventure with it to the publick treasurie, so I entreat leave to try, how I can illustrate that famous monument the hot Bathe water of 𝔅athe, by this engine, before I make use of it on 𝔖tonenge. Suppose then, that when the heathonish Saxons had subdued all this Iland, saving 𝔅athe and parts adjoyning, and at last came so near 𝔅athe as 𝔇ehoram, now 𝔇irram, and having there slain the 3 Kings of 𝔅athe, 𝔊loceſtez and ℭirenceſter, routed their armies, and destroyed those Cities, suppose, I say, upon the invasion of those infidells, and destruction of those Christians, the Lord had, in his wrathfull indignation, dryed up the waters of life and health, as he did ‘other salutiferous waters, upon like provocation, or that Merlin's provecie, *frigebant Badonis balnea, & salubres eorum aquæ mortem generabant,* had been fullfilled, as soon as it had been pronounced; and that those

---

[1] Dr. Ford of the nature and use of the Bathes. Matt. West. pa. 83.

bar-

barbarous Saxons had, in their furie, burnt the Citie to
ashes, and nothing of it remaining, but the old British
names thereof in antient histories, and in the names of
Hills, Rivers, Hamletts, &c. near it, yet much of the
Citie, and nature and propertie of the Bath-water, might
be collected and inferred out of those names now a thousand years afterward; as, first, the tradition of the manner of finding out the vertue of the Bath-water being
this. Bladud, *alias* Bluda, the son and heir of Rudhudibres, beeing smitten with a leprosie, was, Nebuchad-
nezar like, driven out from amongst men, and became
a swineherd near Bathe, which was then a bogg or quagmire of hot water, in which his swine often wallowed,
and one of them, being a Scabbilonian, was thereby
cured, whereupon Bladon making triall of it was also
cured, whereupon he built a Temple, and consecrated it
to the sun, as the God of the heat of the Bath-water,
and Health, which he recovered by the same, and his
father dying, Bladon reigned there in his place. Now
although this is taken generally for a fabulous tradition,
yet much of it may be proved by such old British names,
as aforesaid; as, first, that Bathe was such a bogg, or
quagmire, may be inferred from the most antient name
thereof [1] Car Badon, *the bogg of Bathe,* Meretune, (i. e.)
Mireton.

2. That there was such a King Rudhudibres, may be
inferred from part of his name, still continuing in Rud-
lie, and a relique of his Kinglie dignitie in Kingswood,
Kingsdowne adjoyning.

3. That there was a man of great honour and fame,
living in, or near, Bathe, of the name *Bladon.* For the

1.

---

[1] Matt. West. lib. i⁰.

na-

navigable river, runing under the walls thereof, was called, after his name, Pant=Bladon, and Avon=Bladon,
and *flumen* [1] bladon, (i. e.) *the river of Bladud*, and
the place, where [2] Malmsburie now stands, on the said
River, was called aix=bladon, *the fortified place of Bladud*.

4. That this Bladud was a King, but reduced into
some miserable condition on the North side of Bathe,
as may be collected by his picture over the North gate
of Bathe.

5. That he being healed, as aforesaid, he lived in a
[3] Cave in the side of Salesburie hill there, called *vulgò*
Jackadrum holle, orthog. Jack=cun trwn holl, (i.)
the healed King's hole in the side of the hill, which last
words intimate, that he had some other Cave, in some
other place of the said hill, and about 4 years since there
was discovered a formall Cave, vaulted over with some
Crombs of a man's bones in it, which might be the said
healed King's hole on the topp of the hill, from thence
called *Orthog*. Salut=byl, (f. e.) *health on the topp of the
hill*, in which he might live, die, and be buried in his
own Cave, according to the custome of those dayes, as
Abraham, Sara, &c.

6. That the said Salisburie, being also called Sols
burie, (i. e.) Sunt=burie, (as another little one also, at
the foot thereof, is called Sundaie's hill) the temple of
the sun might be built thereon [4]. For Lantdowne, Lanti=
bridge, and Lambrick, (i. e.) *Temple downe, Templeridge*,
and *Templebridge*, round about this hill, intimate, that
there was such a heathonish temple on it, and what more

---

[1] Guil. Malm. p. 9. [2] Camb. Br. in Belg. [3] *Domus antea
fuerint :* Ovid. Met. lib. 7°. [4] For heathenish temples were built
on high hills. *Hor*.

likely

likely place for *Sol's* temple then 𝕾𝖔𝖑𝖘𝖇𝖚𝖗𝖎𝖊? and why might not that Image of the Sun, like the face of a man, and [1] Hercules, with his Clubb, affixed to the city walls, he brought from 𝕾𝖔𝖑𝖘-𝖇𝖚𝖗𝖎𝖊, as well as those antient Romane urnes there also brought out of the Fields?

7. That, in regard of the supposed influence of the Sun on the 𝕭𝖆𝖙𝖍 water, it was called 𝕾𝖔𝖑-𝖒𝖊𝖗, (*i*) 𝖙𝖍𝖊 𝕾𝖚𝖓-𝕻𝖔𝖔𝖑𝖊, although euphonied into 𝕾𝖔𝖒𝖒𝖊𝖗, as 𝕻𝖘𝖆𝖑𝖒𝖊 into 𝕻𝖘𝖆𝖒𝖊, and 𝕾𝖆𝖑𝖒𝖔𝖓 into 𝕾𝖆𝖒𝖔𝖓, because *Ɫ ante m quiescit.*

8. That, upon the said account, 𝕭𝖆𝖙𝖍𝖊 was antiently called 𝕾𝖔𝖒𝖒𝖊𝖗𝖘𝖊𝖙𝖙, (i. e.) *the seate or Citie of the Sun-poole,* and the province or County of which it was the metropolis, as somtimes *provincia Bathoniensis,* somtimes *Sommersettensis* [2].

9. That the vertue of the 𝕭𝖆𝖙𝖍 water being discovered, as aforesaid, the neighbouring hamlets (as those about 𝕾𝖙𝖔𝖓𝖆𝖌𝖊) ambitiously attributed to themselves variety of names, which they catched, or borrowed, from 𝕭𝖆𝖙𝖍𝖊, as 𝕭𝖆𝖙𝖍𝖊𝖋𝖙𝖔𝖓, 𝕭𝖆𝖙𝖍𝖆𝖒𝖕𝖙𝖔𝖓, 𝕭𝖆𝖙𝖍𝖋𝖔𝖗𝖉, 𝕭𝖆𝖙𝖍𝖜𝖎𝖈𝖐, 𝕭𝖆𝖙𝖍𝖊-𝖉𝖔𝖜𝖓𝖊, &c.

10. That so great was the confluence of people, troubled with aches, to this City, that it was thereupon called 𝕬𝖐𝖊𝖒𝖆𝖓𝖈𝖊𝖋𝖙𝖊𝖗 [3], (i.) *the Citie of ached people.*

11. They esteemed so highly of this water, as the best oyntment for Limbs, as that they termed the City, 𝕻𝖗 𝖊𝖓-𝖓𝖆𝖎𝖓𝖙, *The ointment.*

12. They drank so frequently of this water, that the place was also called, 𝕿𝖜𝖞𝖓𝖒𝖎𝖓, (i. e.) *hot broth.*

13. They raised such multitudes of 𝖍𝖆𝖒𝖘, (i. e.) *home-*

---

[1] Hercules by his 12 labors represents the Sun passing through the 12 signs of the Zodiak. [2] Matt. West. p. 105. [3] Matt. Westm.

ly Cottages, about this water, as that the ground, of large circumference, now without the Citie, is called 𝕭at𝔥am𝔰, 𝕭at𝔥e𝔴ick𝔰𝔥am𝔰, &c. to this day.

14. That this City 𝕭at𝔥am, lying in a low valley, had a 𝕭at𝔥ampton (i. e.) *a Bathefort,* on the toppe of 𝕭at𝔥ampton downe, tó secure the mabout 50 acres off, the topp whereof being surrounded with a strong Dike and Rampire, a sallie port to issue out upon occasion on ℭlau𝔢rton𝔰 downe, and military worke about 100 yeards off, to secure their issues and retreats, and avenue extending from the fort down the hill directly towards 𝕭at𝔥e, whereby the Bathonians might pass and repass securely and invisiblely between 𝕭at𝔥am and 𝕭at𝔥ampton.

15. That, in processe of time, there was so much resort to this hill, that they dwelt here and there over all the downes, which, before inclosures, was comprized all under the name of 𝕭a𝔡on, and, upon that account, 𝕭at𝔥e was also called 𝕭a𝔡on, 𝕭a𝔡onía, 𝕭at𝔥on, 𝕭at𝔥onía, &c.

16. That, for their better security, they afterward fortified the said Downe in more places, as near ℭunlíe Lane end, 𝔚lon𝔡ic𝔥, or ℭ𝔥og-𝔴o𝔡en𝔰𝔡icke, &c. and thereupon it was called ℭair-𝕭a𝔡on, *the fortified Bathedowne.* So that, I say again, if 𝕭at𝔥e had been annihilated 1000 years since, yet these and the like names of it, and other neighbouriug places, preserved, a philantiquarie might easily out of them extract both these, and many more, things, which otherwise would continue buried in oblivion, and much of the fabrick, and many of the names, of 𝔖tonage, and parts and properties thereof, being hitherto preserved, I hope, I shall do the like thereupon, beginning with the first particuler of my conjecture, *viz.*   1. 𝔖tonage

1. Stonage is an old British monument; where, first,
I shall briefly shew, who, and what, the old Britons
were, and afterward, that this was an old British monument.

The old Britons' were the first of six Nations, which
had the possession of this Land successively, *viz. old Britons, Belgæ, Romanes, Saxons, Danes* and *Normans.*
The old Britons came origenally from the Tower of [1] Babell thus. Shortly after the deluge, the Lord having
blessed Noah and his posterity, saying, *be fruitfull, mul-
tiplie aud replenish the earth,* [2] they notwithstanding had
been fruitfull, and had, in a short time, multiplied in-
credibly, yet they obstinately refused to replenish the
earth, but said, *go too, let us build us a Citie and a Tower
in it, whose topp may reach unto heaven, least we be
scattered over the face of the whole earth;* so they intended to dwell in their Citie together, and to secure
themselves from any future flood in the Tower, but the
Lord confounded their one (*viz.* the Hebrew) in 52
Languages, so that they, not understanding each other,
[3] Babling about carrying on the Worke, were necessitated
to give it over unfinished, and then each principall ma i
amongst them having sought out, and brought together,
such as could understand his language, conducted them
into the severall parts of the earth, where many of them
are called after their conducters names to this day, as
the *Medes* from *Madai,* the *Moscovites* from *Mesech*
alias *Mosoch,* the *Canonites* from *Canan,* and *Gomer,*
the eldest son of *Japhet,* calling together all such as
could understand [4] Gomerarg, as the speech of *Gomer,*

---

[1] Camb. Brit. [2] F. *notwithstanding they had.* H. [3] From
whence it was called Babell. Verst. Ant. [4] The Britons of Wales
call their language Comeraeg, to this day.

conducted them to, and seated them in, France, where they were called *Gomeri* after old *Gomer,* and some of them into Britaine. But because [1] he doth not particularize the place, where they were first seated, give me leave to conjecture, that it was in 𝔐𝔬𝔲𝔫𝔱 𝔊𝔬𝔪𝔢𝔯𝔦 in Wales (for that is also called 𝔗𝔯𝔢𝔣𝔞𝔩𝔡𝔤𝔲𝔦𝔫, *the famous old Towne,* a proper name for such old Towns-men.) From 𝔐𝔬𝔲𝔫𝔱 𝔊𝔬𝔪𝔢𝔯𝔦 they might dilate their plantation over all 𝔐𝔬𝔲𝔫𝔱 𝔊𝔬𝔪𝔢𝔯𝔦𝔰𝔥𝔦𝔯𝔢, still called *Gomori,* as long as they had such garments [2] as their fore-fathers had; but those being worne out, and they being destitute (in this wilderness) of meanes to recruite apparrell, yet found expedients to paint their naked bodies with severall Coullers of Cloathes, and then they were no longer called *Gomeri,* but *Britons,* (i. e.) *Painters,* and their land *Britaine,* (i. e.) *the painted nation* [3]. Some families painted 𝔤𝔴𝔦𝔫 *white,* some 𝔡𝔲 *black,* some 𝔊𝔩𝔞𝔰 *blew,* some 𝔊𝔬𝔠𝔥 (pronounced 𝔊𝔬𝔣𝔣) *red,* some 𝔏𝔩𝔬𝔦𝔡 (pronounced 𝔉𝔩𝔬𝔶𝔡) *green,* and this is the originall of those common names 𝔊𝔴𝔦𝔫, 𝔡𝔲, 𝔊𝔩𝔞𝔰, 𝔊𝔬𝔣𝔣 and 𝔉𝔩𝔬𝔶𝔡, amongst their posteritie in Wales to this day. He that desires any farther intelligence concerning the old Britons, let him reade Cæsar's Commentaries, Strabo, Diodorus Siculus, Pomponius Mela, Solinus, Dio Cassius, Ziphiline, Plinius Secundus, Cambden, Speede, &c.

Having seen who the old Britons were, we may, in the next place, well look upon this 𝔖𝔱𝔬𝔫𝔞𝔤𝔢 as an old British monument. If it had but one old British name, it were a probable argument, that it was an old British thing. For *conveniunt rebus nomina, ut supra.* For who, but old British Founders, would have given it an

---

[1] Camb. Brit.   [2] Gen. 9.   [3] Camb. Brit. de prim. incol.

old

old British name? But if I can produce, at least, old
British names thereof, and parts and properties thereof,
and not one Belgick, Romane, Saxon, Deanish or Nor-
man name thereof (but the nick-name ' 𝔖𝔱𝔬𝔫𝔠𝔥𝔢𝔫𝔤𝔢)
then, surely, it was an old British monument. I forbear
mentioning those names now, because I would not tau-
tologize, when I shall have occasion both to mention
and interpret sometimes one, sometimes another, of
them. But the Architector (and I wish I could say the
Antiquarie) Jones is point blanck against a British, and
also for a Romane, Monument, and I will complie with
him, as farr as I may, by saying, it might be a Romane
work, but not a Romane Monument. For it is true,
which he mainteins at large, that this monument was
framed according to the most exquesite rules of Architecture, in which the pittifull naked Britons had no
knowledge at all, and the Romans were the most expert
men in the world in that art, and might be hired by the
Britons to do that work for them. For ² there was a
commerce between the Britons and forreigne nations,
before Julius Cæsar's dayes, insomuch that the Græcians
frequented this Iland upon this account; and if so, then
much more the nearer and more Architectonicall Romanes, who as they ³ taught and helped the Britons to
build tempells after they had conquered them (being
well hired,) so might some of them build, or help them
to build, this one before they conquered them, and, in
this respect, it might be called a Roman work, but no
more a Romane Monument, or Temple, then the temple of the Jews might be called the temple of the Gen-

---

' (*I. e.*) *Stone hanging place*, because some remaines of it are
like gallowes. ² Cæs. Com. lib. 5. ³ Cornelius Tacitus.

s 3 tiles,

tiles, because the Gentiles had the chiefest hand in building it for the Jews. The Romans endeavoured (no way more, then) by magnificent Structures to perpetuate their fame, as well in this Iland, as in other places, and, to this end, they imposed their Romane names on them, as *Templum Claudii; ac Camalodunum,* consecreated *Victoriæ; murus Severi,* extending from Sea to Sea in the North of this Land; the fosse way from the Roman *fossa,* a ditch on each side of it, out of which the earth was cast up; [1] *Antonini Itinerarium,* by which he devided Britaine into 16 *Itinera,* and every *Iter* into 12, 13 or 14 Mansions, some Remainders of some of them to be seen to this day. Not so much as that paltrie tottering bridge, built by, or for, the Romanes, near Glaſſenbuʒʒe, but must be called by the Romane name *Pons periculosus,* and is called Pomperiʒ at this day, and if so, then, surely, this most glorious monument (if it had been Roman) should have been called after the name of one of the Roman Emperors, as [2] founders of it, at least by some other Roman name or word; but no Roman name, word or syllable, on or near it, but all British, is *argumentum Herculissimum,* that it was no Roman, but a British, monument.

2. My second particuler is, that a bloody battle was foughten at Stonage. For the very name Stoneage, signifies *Stone-battle,* the last syllable age comeing from [3] the Greek ἀγών, *a furious battle,* and a village near Stonage is called Fittle-ton, not in regard of it's owne

---

[4] See Burton's Com. on it. [2] F. *founder.* H. [3] When the Græcians came and traded with the Britons, they left some part of their words compounded with British, as Iſis, Thamaſis, age in Stonage. Camb. Brit. in Belg: Speede.

Si-

Situation (in a valley;) but because it is near the *fight-* *tullton,* or *place* [1] *hired in, where the fight was,* (i. e.) **Stonage,** which stand in the midst of a multitude of burrowes, *(i. e.)* burying hillocks, which are the *tumuli* or tombes, in which the slaine of the battle were buried. He that can not, or will not, believe it, let him scearch one of them, and there see the fragments of mens bones, and peices of their old fashoned armour, spoken of by Cambden, Speede, &c. and conclude, as I do, this particuler, that all, that have built their opinion of this monument, on any other foundation, then a bloody battle, have built **Stonages** in the aire.

8. This bloudie battle produced a glorious Victorie. It was not *bellum anceps,* or a drawn battle. He that runeth may reade almost clear Victorie of the one over the other armie, in the numerous traines of burrowes, with mens bones in them, extending from **Stonage** to **Amesburie,** and from thence to the topp of **Haradon hill,** about 5 miles in all the burrowes, being very great, and standing thicke at, and near, **Stonage,** and still smaller and thinner till near the topp of **Haradon hill,** plainly declaring the great execution done neare **Stonage,** and that the conquered Armie fled toward **Haradon hill,** the conquering armie pursued them thither, and slew many thousands of them, and buried them in heaps together, in, and near, London way to the said hill.

4. That this Victorie was won by the *Cangi* of **Glad-er-haf,** *viz.* the people of Sommersett, who [2] where all called *Cangi* [3], (i. e.) *Singers to instruments of Musick,* from [4] **Canig,** *Canticum organi musici,* in which, it

---

[1] F. *buried.* H. [2] Sic. *H.* [3] Camb. Brit. in Belg. ex Tacito. [4] Dr. Davis Dic. Brit. Lat.

seems, they delighted so much, that, as the old Britons did, so their posteritie of Wales do, call Sommersett Glad-er-bat, *the merry Summer-field,* to this day. The *Cangi* then were the Westermost inhabitants of this Iland. For Devon and Cornwall were not then inhabited, and their province extended East-ward either to, or near unto, Stonage. For Mr. Cambden [1] intimateth, that Cannings Hundred, reaching within few miles of Stonage, was so called, as being part of the *Cangies* territories, [2] whence I inferr, that if the traine of burying billocks aforesaid, had extended from Stonage westward, then the *Cangi* had been routed and slaine in their flight home-ward. But the traine extending East-ward declareth, that the *Cangi,* coming out of their westerne parts, routed their enemies assoone as they began to enter upon their frontiers, and pursued them East-ward towards their homes, or quarters, as more in due place.

5. That these *Cangi* were Giants will appear,

1. by their names. For Cambden [3], Speed, &c. affirme, that this monument was antiently called *the Giants dance,* and Cannings or the [4] Cangings, near Stonage, signifie Cangick Giants.

2. By their chaines, intimated by all the names of Rivers and Villages on them near Stonage, which have the syllable *in* or *yng* in them [5]. For they come from Heb. [6] Anak, which signifies *a Giant hanging a Chain about his neck,* as those Anakims in the scripture, and such Anakims were the Gigantick old Britons, wearing Chaines about their necks and wasts. [7] *vestis usum non*

---

[1] Camb. in Belg.   [2] *Whenche* MS. *H.*   [3] Camb. in Belg.
[4] *Cangings* MS. *H.*   [5] Dr. Davis his Dic. Br. Lat.   [6] Leighe's Crit. Sac. p. 373. and Ainsworth Ps. 736.   [7] Herodian. pa. 106.

                                                    cogno-

cognorunt, ventrem atque cervicem ferro incingunt, or-
namentum id esse, ac divitiarum argumentum, existi-
mantes, and thus pride compassed them about as a chaine
' Psalm lxxiii.

3. By some huge bones of men, found, amongst others,
in the said burrowes, as aforesaid, and in other places near
𝔖tonage, according to the very words of Sr. Thomas Elliott in his Dictionarie, on the word *Gigas.* 𝔄bout 30
pears since 𝔍 mp self, being with mp father, 𝔖r. 𝔕i-
chard Elliott, at a 𝔐onasterie of regular Canons (three
or four miles from 𝔖tonage,) beheld the bones of a
dead man found deep in the ground, which being joyn-
ed together, was in length ² 13 foot and 10 inches,
whereof one of the teeth mp father had, which was of
the quantity of a great wallnut. 𝔗his 𝔍 have written. (saith he) because some men will beleive nothing,
that is out of the compass of their own knowledge.
He that cannot beleive Sir Thomas Elliott, let him see a
Giant's tooth, which I can shew him, diged up *Anno*
Domini 1670. at 𝔚eedmoore near 𝔚ells, three inches
long above the roots, 3 inches about, and 4 ounces in
weight, and at the Lord Sturton's house in 𝔖turton
Caundell, (i. e.) *the borders of the Cangi,* a Giant's
thigh bone of a full yeard, in which instances argue, that,
as amongst the Canonites, so amongst the conquering
Cangi, there were races of Giants 10 principall Com-
manders, in regard of which 𝔖tonage was called *Giants*
Dance. For *Denominatio sumitur à præstantiori.* Arist.
Organ.

' *Psalm* xxx. *By* &c. MS. without either the figure of 3, or beginning a new Paragraph. *H.* ² 'Tis xiiii. in some Editions of
Elyot. *H.*

4. by

4. by their armour, or peices of it, (which, when new, was large enough for Giants) found there also. But

5. here I must distinguish Giants into two sorts, Giants of antiquitie, and Giants of abilitie, and so declare what sort of these 2 the *Cangi* were. Giants of antiquity were so called in respect of their senioritie, as if they had not been borne into the world by the way of all flesh. For they being heathens, and not beleiving any Creation, supposed the first inhabitants of each nation, were brought forth by the earth, as froggs, mice, serpents, and hereupon the earth was worshiped by the name of *Dea mater*, and the first inhabitants termned *Terræ filii*, and *terrâ editi*, and *Gigantes*, (à γίνομαι ετ γαῖα, Dorice γᾶ) that is, *men brought forth by the earth*, according to that of the Poet [1]:

> *Terra feros partus, immania monstra Gigantes,*
> *Edidit.*

And such were the Giants of antiquity. Giants of ability were men of a very great stature and strength. And these Cangick Conquerors were Giants both of great Antiquitie and Abilitie. Their great Antiquitie may appear in 𝔄llyngton, *orthog.* 𝔄lðínton, (i. e.) *antient Giants ton*. Their abilitie in 𝔄blíngton, (i. e.) *able* or *strong Giants-ton*. For neither of these two names were proper to either of those villages, but borrowed from 𝔖tonage as aforesaid, and now restored to 𝔖tonage, to declare the antiquity and ability of the Cangick Giants, which here conquered. As *ex ungue Leonem*, so *ex dente Gigantem*, it is easie to conjecture at the incredible stature

---

[1] Ovid. Meta.

and

and strength of a Cangick Giant, by the topp of his skull an inch thick, and a tooth of his, which I have, 3 inches long[1] now since the root is broken away, and three inches and a quarter round, and three ounces and half in weight, being full four ounces till the roots were broken off; so that, according to this instance, the Cangick Giants were very much greater and stronger then Goliah, or any other of the Giants described in the Scripture. Mr. Cambden writes of two teeth of a Giant, out of which 200 ordinary teeth might be cut, and this one Cheektooth weigheth just 100 Cheek teeth.

6. That the commander in chase of these *Cangi* was the famous old [2] *Stanenges* of Glad=ar=haf aforesaid, which gives demonstration age, as Stonage was one, so Stanenges another, Britannick-Græcian name of this Monument, compounded of Stane and ἐγγὺς, (i. e.) *Stones pitched up near together;* and as Stanenges was the name of this antient Monument, so also of a most antient family flourishing in Glad=ar=haf to this day, which name could not arise from any other place, or thing, then this monument. For there was never any other place, or thing, of this name but this.

Therefore, the prime Ancestour, of the family *Stanenges*, took his name from this monument Stonenges, which being easily granted, it will be enquired, upon what account he took his name from this monument? and answered, it must be either from his [3] habitation there, or from some action performed there by him.

---

[1] These reliques of a Cangick Giant, were found 13 foot deep in digging of a draught well, in Meumore, *Anno Domini* 1670. [2] H. Hun. lib. primo Histor. [3] As Hill Daletwood, Meabe field, &c. were so called from their dwelling in such places.

Not

Not from any inhabitation there. For it was an heathenish Temple, as shall be shewed, and the inhabiting in, or at, it had been esteemed a greater prophanation, then the dwelling in a Church or Chappell. Besides, there was no water, nor any other accommodation for a dwelling, within 2 or 3 miles of it. So the name of 𝔖𝔱𝔞𝔫𝔢𝔫𝔤𝔢𝔰 was not taken from any habitation there, but from some action performed there; and what action could that be, but from conquering, and erecting this Trophie there? Nimrod the conquerour, and his adherents, would needs build him a 'Bable to get him a name, and from what else could Trophimus, and others of that name before and since him, take their Tropicall names, but from their Trophies? And why should not old *Stanenges* take his name from 𝔖𝔱𝔞𝔫𝔢𝔫𝔤𝔢𝔰 also; as he did his Arms, 3 Batts volitant in a field argent, from the innumerable multitude of Batts (the peculiar animals of that place) ambuscadeing there by day, and rendevouzing by night, never so much as any sheep coming to rubbe or shelter there. Or in what respect could their most antient 𝔥𝔬𝔫𝔫𝔦-𝔠𝔲𝔱𝔱, *alias* 𝔥𝔬𝔫𝔫𝔦𝔞𝔡-𝔠𝔲𝔱𝔱, (i, e.) *illustrious court*, be so called, but from that most antient illustrious *Stanenges* of 𝔥𝔬𝔫𝔫𝔦𝔠𝔲𝔱𝔱, who wonne the field, and erected the Trophie aforesaid?

7. The people conquered by the *Cangi* were King *Divitiacus* and his *Belgæ* of Low Germanie. For

1. The king *Divitiacus* and his *Belgæ* were the only people recorded, that invaded the old Britons, and therefore if the old Britons conquered such as invaded them, they were the King *Divitiacus* and his *Belgæ*.

' No monument was ever erected, but to gett the owner a name.

2. Ju-

2. Julius Cæsar saith, that ' *Divitiacus magnum partem Britanniæ obtinebat nostrâ etiam memoriâ;* which great part of Britaine Mr. Cambden supposeth was Hampshire, Wiltshire, and Sommersett, called antiently the *Belgæ,* after the name of those which conquered them ; but Julius Cæsar doth not say, they conquered them without any repulse. Julius Cæsar himself was routed 2 or 3 times by the Britons, before he could subdue that little part of Britaine which he did, and therefore King *Divitiacus* and his *Belgæ* might be routed, at least, once by them, and at 𝔖tonage, before they could *vincere* that great part of Britaine called *Belgæ.*

3. The armie, which was conquered, fled Northeast directly towards *Belgium,* as the traine of Burrowes aforesaid declares.

4. 𝔥arabun 𝔥ill, *orthog.* 𝔥ertobun, to which the routed armie fled for refuge, is a Belgick word, or name, signifying *the hill of refuge.* and who was so likely as the *Belgæ,* to give it a Belgick name of refuge, when being routed at 𝔖tonage, they fled back thither for refuge? all which being put together, will amount to some such historie, insteade of a Chronicle, as this:

Divitiacus, King of the *Belgæ,* invading Britaine with his *Salii* of *Belgium,* came into Wiltshire, and quartered and plundered all over the Salisburie Plaine, particularly at 𝔖alethorpe, 𝔏urgſſale, 𝔯uſſiſale, ² 𝔐artinſale, 𝔐artinſale, 𝔏uſſale, &c. so called from the *Salii,* which were the chief people of the *Belgæ.* Old *Stenenges* and his *Cangi* drew up their Armie in 𝔓earnsburie, *orth.* 𝔓amaithburie, 𝔠aſtle, 5 miles Westward from 𝔖ton.

6 𝔖alſ round about 𝔖tonage, and not one more in a Wilts, Hampis. Somersett, or Dorsett.

' Cæsar's Com. Lib. 5.   ² Sic. *II.*

age,

age, *Divitiacus* and his armie from the topp of 𝔥𝔞𝔯𝔞-
𝔡𝔬𝔫 𝔥𝔦𝔩𝔩 5 miles Northeast thereof, where, after they
had faced each other a while, they mett and fought a
bloudie battle in the midd-way, where the *Belgæ* being
routed, fled homeward toward their said hill of refuge,
but so many of their *Saxi* were slain and buried in the
burrowes aforesaid, that the field was ever since called
𝔖𝔞𝔩𝔦𝔰𝔟𝔲𝔯𝔦𝔢 𝔓𝔩𝔞𝔦𝔫𝔢.

   8. The Cangick Giants having conquered, triumphed
over their enemies at 𝔖𝔱𝔬𝔫𝔞𝔤𝔢, which, upon that occasion, was called *the Giants dance*, and this triumphant
singing and dancing together, at the time and place of
Victorie, was the common practice of the antients. So
when [1] Jephtha had conquered the Ammonites, the Israelites triumphed with timbrell and dances. So assoone as
[2] David had slain Goliah, and the Philistines were routed, the Isralites triumphed, singing and dancing with
Tabretts and joy, and with instruments of Musick, and
the women answered one to another as they played, *Saul
hath slain his thousands, and David his ten thousands.*
So assoon as the Lord had given victorie to the Isralites
over the Egyptians, and that they saw the Egyptians
dead upon the Sea shore, [3] *Then sang Moses and the
Children of Israell this song unto the Lord* &c. and then
verss the 20th. *Miriam the Prophetess, the sister of Aa-
ron, took a timbrell in her hand, and all the women went
out after her with Tabretts and with dances, and Miriam answered them, sing ye to the Lord, for he hath
triumphed gloriously.* And yet not long [4] after they sang
and danced a *palinodia,* like an herd of skipping and

---

[1] Judges the 11th.   [2] 1 Sam. 18. 6.   [3] Exodus 15. 1.
[4] Exodus 32. and the 8.

                                  bleating

bleating Calves, *to the similitude of a* [1] *Calf that* [2] *eatheth hay, sitting down to eat and drink, and riseing up t. play,* dancing and singing, (much out of Tune) *these be thy Gods, O Israell, which have brought* [3] *the up out of the land of Egypt,* and this Idolatrous singing and dancing being too easily learned of the Gentiles from the Jewes, was put in practice at 𝔖tonage, by the Cangick Giants of 𝔊lað-ꜩ-ɧaꜩ, which was thereupon called *the Giants dance.*

9. But all this singing and dancing did but beate the aire, uncapable of any legible impression, in which, posteritie might read this glorious victorie; therefore they thought it expedient to erect this Monument, as their [4] Trophie, and as such a Gazett, as all the world might gaze at, and in it admire their Heroicall valour through all generations: and herein also they imitated, or rather emulated, the Isralites, who being delivered from the Egyptians, and having trampled the Red Sea and Jordan (opposing them) under their feet, did, by God's command, erect a 𝔖tonage of twelve Stones in the midst of Jordan, whence it was driven back, and they are [5] there, saith Josuah [6], unto this day, standing, perhaps, as a circuler guard of Souldiers, up to their middle in water, as keeping in possession what had been conquered as aforesaid; and another such a 𝔖tonage of 12 Stones they carried to their first quarters, and erected them as a memoriall to the Children of Israell for ever. vers. 7.

---

[1] Psalm. 106. ver. 20. &c. [2] Sic. *II.* [3] Sic. *H.* [4] A τρέφω, *to turne,* because it was set at the place, where their Enemies were turned to flight, at the beginning of the traine of the Burrowes aforesaid, &c. [5] *They* MS. *H.* [6] Joshua the 4th 8th.

This

This Trophie of these Giants was called 𝔐anuyng, *orthogr.* ' 𝔐anyng, (i. e.) *Giants great Stone,* observable in the 3 𝔐anyng fords, so called, because at each of those villages there are fords to pass over that River, which runeth downe near to 𝔐anyng, or *Giants great Stones.* So that although that River is commonly called 𝔄von (i. e.) *the River,* yet the proper name is 𝔐anyng, *the Giants great Stones,* from runing downe near them, as 𝔑ormanton, *orth.* 𝔑orthmanton, (i. e.) *the Towne standing nearest to them;* and all this may be exemplified by other old British Trophies, all resembling 𝔖tonage in theire circuler formes, British names, and some other respects, although not in magnificence, as

1. The first was also called 𝔐anton near Marlburrowe, from a pettie 𝔖tonage there, of eight huge Stones, now called *the broad Stones,* antiently standing, but now lying circularly in London way, testified to be a British Trophie, by the fragments of mens bones found in the Burrowes in the fields adjoyning.

2. On 𝔖evenburrowes hill, 4 Miles West of Marleburrow near London way, are 40 great Stones, sometimes standing, but now lying in a large Circle, inclosing an inner circle of 16 great Stones, now lying also, testified to be an old British Trophie by the Anglo-British name thereof, *(viz.) Seaven Burrowes,* and by those 7 huge Burrowes very near it with fragments of mens bones.

3. At 𝔖tanton 𝔇ru, six miles on the South of Bristoll, are 8 Stones bigger then the greatest of those at 𝔖tonage, but their topps broken off, so that they are

---

' 𝔐an signifies such a great stone as a piller, milstone &c. from which the British proverb 𝔈aleclach girin, as man: *durior est fortis quam saxum.*

not

not above 12 foot high standing circulerlie, and round about, within 200 yeard of those 8, are, at least, 60 more smaller stones, 6, 7 or 8 foot high, standing upright.

This was an old British Trophie, as may appear by the name thereof, reteined still in the name of the parrish, in which it stands, *viz.* Stanton-Dꞩu, *the Stone Town of Victorie.* 2 by the smaller stones, monuments of the Conquerours friends [1] their slain, one of which being lately fallen, in the Pitt, in which it stood, were found the crumbes of a man's bones, and a round bell, like a large horse-bell, with a skrew as the stemme of it; whence I conjecture, that as the circle of large Stones was the Trophie of victorie, so those smaller were monuments of friends slain in wining the Victorie, (for Victors would not honour their enemies with such monuments:) and the bell was part of an old Briton's Weapon, there buried with it's owner, and, I suppose, the like bones and bells may be found under the other small stones, confirming the præmisces. For Mr. Speed, in his Chronicle, pictureth an old Briton naked, Lions, Beares, Serpents painted on him to terrifie enemies, [2] with a Lance in his hand, on the butt end whereof is such a bell screwed fast, which served in steade of a Trumpett to alarme, and a clubb to dash out the enemies braines, and this bell was, I suppose, the permanent part of that old Briton's weapon there buried with his owner, according to the old custome, continued to this day, in burying Souldiers weapons with them, at least in carrying them on their Coffins to their graves.

---

[1] Sic. *H.* [2] Herodianus.

4. In Denbigh shire ' is a famous monument of a cir-
cle of great Stones, called **Cereg y Drusion**, (i. e.) *the
Stones of Victorie,* alias *the stones of the Druides,* (i. e.)
Priests sacryficeing at Victories.

5. In Mount Gomerie Shire [2] there is an high Mountain, called **Cornbon**, on which there is a famous monument of great stones, standing circulerly, a Trophie of
Victory.

6. At **Biscaw Waum** in Cornwall [3] are 21 great
Stones in a Circle, the greatest standing in the Center,
a Trophie of Victorie.

7. At **Hochfnorton** in Oxford Shire [4] 36 very great
stones in a circle, called **Roll-rich-stones**, and this, as all
the former, deemed Trophies of Victorie, by that Ora-
cle of antiquities Mr. Cambden, who, for the excellen-
cie of his knowledge in affaires of this Nature, was
created King at armes, and if all these pettie, or dimi-
nitive, **Stonages** were Trophies of Victorie, then, surely, their great grandfather **Stonage** was a Trophie of
that Victorie aforesaid.

Q. But what kind of Stones are they? how brought
hither? and sett up in this place?

A. *Quot homines tot sententiæ,* the first is, that monstrous legend of Monmouth, and his Giants bringing
them *per mare, per terras,* out of the utmost parts of
Africa, to **Kilbare,** &c. of which a little, but too much,
already.

2. The second is, that childish tale of Childrie, who,
because he could find no small stones on Salisburie

/

' Camb. Brit. in Ordov.   ² Camb. Brit.   ³ Cam. Brit. in
Cornwall.   Cam. Brit. in Oxford shire.

plaines,

plaines, dreamed [1], that nature had aggregated all the la-
pidificke Vertue of that country into 𝔖tonage.

3. The third is, that of Inigo [2], who might truly have
said *out I goe,* when, after he had affirmed, fol. [3] 10.
they were hewen out of a quarrie at 𝔄𝔰burie, he said,
they are so churlish and extream hard, that they disdaine
the touch of tooles, and if they were hewne out from
thence, tell me, how they were brought 15 miles over
hills and dales from thence to 𝔖tonage, & *eris mihi
magnus Apollo.*

4. The fourth is, that of learned Cambden, who supposeth [4] them to be *saxa factitia ex arena pura &* [5] *un-
ctuoso aliquo coagmentata.*

5. And I am confident they are *saxa factitia,* great
artificial stones, made of many small naturall Stones,
[6] made of many small naturall Stones". That a Lime-
kilne was there erected, which being filled with lime-
stones, extraordinarily coaled, were melted with fer-
vent heat into a birdlime-like substance, which was let
runne out into such variety of Cisterns, one after another, as formed them for their severall places, into which
they were drawne up by some Crane, or other Engine.

1. My reasons are; first, itt was impossible to work
them into their severall formes. Free stones may be
wrought to any, but these churlish stones to no, forme,
in regard of hardness and brittleness.

2. Iron [7] ginnes, chimney back-stones, stone-inges,
the pillers of the late royall exchange, the 8 great pillers
of 𝔖tanton-𝔇ru Trophie, were all cast stones, formed

[1] In his Brit. Bac. [2] Inigo Jones in his Stonehenge restored.
[3] L. 36. *H.* [4] Camb. in Belg. edit. 4ª. [5] *Unctuoquo* MS.
II. [6] F. delend. *II.* [7] *Ginmes* MS. *II.*

T 2 *some*

some of one, some of another, sort of melted stones, and why might not Stonage-stones be so also? Surely heere was such an aggregation for a saxification, but not made by Minerva, as Childrie doteth, but Mars, or indeed by the Martiall old Britons, who having been active in gaining the victorie, were officious in gathering together the small stones of the plaines to be melted into great ones, and so *multorum manibus grande levatur onus,* an old British limeburner and his stonegetherers performed this *opus herculissimum.*

10. This trophie was a Temple, or rather a Tropicall Temple. For first, it was the common practice of the heathens, to promise and vow Temples as Trophies to their supposed Gods, or Goddessess, of Victorie, in case they would give them some great Victorie, which when they had obtained, they surely built it accordingly in the place aforesaid of an ordinarie Trophie, so it was called a Tropicall Temple, and, upon this account, the Romans usuallie vowed and built Temples as Trophies to Mars, Victoria, &c. and upon this account Canutus built [1] a Temple at Aſh Downe, and all other places where he wone Victories; yea some Christians have imitated heathens in this particuler, as King William the Conqueroyr, once, though he built not a Temple to Mars, yet he did an Abbey to St. Martin, as a Trophie, in the place where he conquered King Herald, the ruines whereof in Sussex are called Battle abbey to this day.

2. Stonage was a Temple in respect of the magnificence thereof. Any such circle of rough stones, as aforesaid, served well enough for a Trophie, but this was a magnificent Tropicall Temple, or Templarie Trophie.

---

[1] Camb. Brit. in Essex.

3. Stonage

3. Stonage was of a Circuler forme, according to the forme of all other heathonish Temples.

4. In that it stood *sub·dio*, open to the heavens and ayre. For the Heathens [1] accounted it a great sin to imprison their Gods within roofs and walls, who would have liberty (as they thought) to be abroad doing good.

5. It was the opinion of our great Architector [2] (orthodox in this point) saying, I am clearly of opinion, that Stonage was originally a Temple.

6. Wilton, within 2 miles of Stonage, was antiently called Llandune (pronounced Ellandune) (i.) *Temple-downe*, not in regard of any such thing in it self, but in regard it was so near the said heathonish Temple, and the Earles of Wiltshire were antiently stiled Earles of Ellandune, and if Wilton, the old Metropolis of Wiltshire, took it's antient name from this Temple, then consequently Wiltshire, and all the rest of the Wills about Stonage, as Willibourne, Willfall, Willford, and Wilsford, Wilcott, and Willcot situate some on one, some on other, of the Rivers near Stonage, took their Templarie names from, and must then restore them to, Stonage, to prove that it was a Temple, and so must all those Villages near it, whose names begin with Chel or [4] Clil, which antiently were Cel and Cill, signifying, properlie, *the Cell of a Temple*, but here synecdochichallie (the chief part for the whole) *a Temple;* so that, according to the rule aforesaid, Chilton termeth Stonage *a Temple,* Chelterton *an elegant Temple,* but Chelterinton *the Giants elegant Temple.* And if Stonage was such a triumphant Tropicall Temple of singing and

---

[1] Godw. Anti. [2] Inigo Jones, pa. 75. [3] Camb. Brit. in Belg. [4] F. Chil. *H.*

danceing,

danceing, then, surely, no such sepulchre of sorrow, or
monument of mourning, weeping, wailing and gnashing
of teeth, erected by the old Britons for Aurelius Ambrosius, according to *Polydorus Virgilius*, or for the old
Britons by Aurelius Ambrosius, according to *Galfridus
Monumethensis*, or for Queen Baodicea by the *Iceni*,
according to *Anonimus*. For never any sepulchre bare
any aspect like this monument, but far different in forme,
manner and composure. The severall pillers of Rachell
and Absolon, the [1] columnes of Vespatian and Trajane,
the one having his shield, the other a Colossus on the
topp of it, had no resemblance with this. Neither had
the *Obelisks* of *Mitres* or *Ramesis*, or the *Piramides
of Memphis*, or *Arsinoe*, or the *Mausoleum* of *Arthe-
misia*, any resemblance with Sfonage. And how much
did the sepulchre of King Arthur, [2] buried at Glaſtenbu-
rie in an hallowed Oake, with a little *Pyramis* at the
head, and another at the feet, differ from this? Is there
any probability, that King Arthur and Ambrosius, fellow Christians, Coætanians, living and dying so near
together in time and place, that the one should be buried and monumented according to the custome of the
old British Kings and Princes, and the other as never
man before, or since? Amongst all nations sepulchres
were alwaies such sollid piles, as might be truly termed
monuments, (*i. e.*) remaines, not ayerious, with fre-
quent openings and void spaces within, and subject to
ruine, but this was such, therefore no sepulchre, but a
Temple.

11. And this Temple was consecrated to *Andraste*,
aliàs *Anraith*, aliàs *Andates*, their Goddess of Victorie.

---

[1] Plin. Secund. pa. 249.   [2] Cam. in Belg.

For

For to whome else would, or could, they dedicate a
Temple for Victorie, but to their supposed Goddesse
of Victorie? She was termed *Andraste,* in relation to
the Conquerors, from [1] ἄνδραι᷉⊕·, a manlie *virago,* not
quasi, but *quia, vir agens,* playing the man, and, in respect of the conquered, *Anraith.* For as 𝔯𝔥𝔞𝔦𝔡 signified
a Spear, so 𝔄𝔫𝔯𝔞𝔦𝔡 and 𝔄𝔫𝔯𝔞𝔦𝔱𝔥 *unseparated,* figura-
tively *disarmed and bereft of all treasures, garments,*
food and other necessaries to maintaine life; and it is
observable, that some parts of those names, *Andraste,*
Anraith and *Andates,* are retained in the names of some
of the circumjacent Villages to this day;

1. as 𝔄𝔫𝔡𝔯𝔞𝔰𝔱𝔢 in 𝔄𝔫𝔡𝔯𝔬𝔰𝔥 𝔏𝔲𝔫𝔰𝔡𝔬𝔫. There is a 𝔅𝔢𝔯=
𝔯𝔦 𝔅𝔩𝔲𝔫𝔰𝔡𝔬𝔫, a broade 𝔅𝔩𝔲𝔫𝔰𝔡𝔬𝔫, and an 𝔄𝔫𝔡𝔯𝔬𝔰𝔥 𝔏𝔲𝔫𝔰=
𝔡𝔬𝔫, and 𝔄𝔫𝔡𝔯𝔬𝔰𝔥 𝔏𝔲𝔫𝔰𝔡𝔬𝔫 is nearest to the Temple of
Andraste; two 𝔒𝔤𝔟𝔲𝔯𝔫𝔢𝔰, 𝔊𝔢𝔬𝔯𝔤𝔢 𝔒𝔤𝔟𝔲𝔯𝔫𝔢, and 𝔄𝔫=
𝔡𝔯𝔬𝔰 𝔒𝔤𝔟𝔲𝔯𝔫𝔢, nearest to this Temple of *Andraste;*
3 [2] 𝔆𝔞𝔩𝔩𝔦𝔫𝔤𝔟𝔲𝔯𝔫𝔢, 𝔆𝔞𝔩𝔩𝔦𝔫𝔤𝔟𝔬𝔲𝔯𝔫𝔢, 𝔆𝔞𝔩𝔩𝔦𝔫𝔤𝔟𝔲𝔯𝔫𝔢 𝔎𝔦𝔫𝔤=
𝔰𝔱𝔬𝔫, and 𝔆𝔞𝔩𝔩𝔦𝔫𝔤𝔟𝔲𝔯𝔫𝔢 𝔄𝔫𝔡𝔯𝔬𝔰, and 𝔆𝔞𝔩𝔩𝔦𝔫𝔤𝔟𝔲𝔯𝔫 𝔄𝔫=
𝔡𝔯𝔬𝔰 nearest to this Temple of Andraste. The name of 2.
𝔄𝔫𝔯𝔞𝔦𝔱𝔥 is retained in 𝔓𝔞𝔯𝔫𝔰𝔟𝔲𝔯𝔦𝔢 𝔆𝔞𝔰𝔱𝔩𝔢, (*orthog.* ɏ 𝔄𝔫=
𝔯𝔞𝔦𝔱𝔥𝔰𝔟𝔲𝔯𝔦𝔢 𝔆𝔞𝔰𝔱𝔩𝔢,) in 𝔊𝔯𝔢𝔞𝔱 𝔄𝔪𝔢𝔰𝔟𝔲𝔯𝔦𝔢 and 𝔏𝔦𝔱𝔱𝔩𝔢
𝔄𝔪𝔢𝔰𝔟𝔲𝔯𝔦𝔢, [3] wich Mr. Speede, in his Mapp, termns
𝔄𝔫𝔰𝔟𝔲𝔯𝔦𝔢, (*i. e.*) 𝔄𝔫𝔯𝔞𝔦𝔱𝔥𝔰𝔟𝔲𝔯𝔦𝔢, so distinguished from
ɏ 𝔄𝔫𝔯𝔞𝔦𝔱𝔥𝔰𝔟𝔲𝔯𝔦𝔢 𝔆𝔞𝔰𝔱𝔩𝔢, and upon the same account the
two 𝔄𝔫𝔰𝔱𝔦𝔢𝔰 and 𝔄𝔫𝔰 𝔥𝔦𝔩𝔩𝔰 might be 𝔄𝔫𝔯𝔞𝔦𝔱𝔥𝔰𝔱𝔦𝔢 and
𝔄𝔫𝔯𝔞𝔦𝔱𝔥𝔰 𝔥𝔦𝔩𝔩, but euphonied to what they are now, because they did stick in the teeth in pronunciation. 𝔄𝔫= 3.
𝔡𝔞𝔱𝔢𝔰 in 𝔄𝔫𝔡𝔬𝔟𝔢𝔯, (*orthog.* 𝔄𝔫𝔡𝔴𝔣𝔲𝔯,) 𝔄𝔫𝔡𝔞𝔱𝔢𝔰 river runing through it, and 𝔄𝔫𝔡𝔢𝔳𝔢𝔯𝔩𝔢𝔶 𝔥𝔲𝔫𝔡𝔯𝔢𝔡; so that whereas

---

[1] Sic, pro ἀνδρεῖος. *II.*   [2] F. 𝔆𝔞𝔩𝔩𝔦𝔫𝔤𝔟𝔲𝔯𝔫𝔢𝔰. *II.*   [3] Sic. *II.*

T 4   onlie

onlie 4 parrishes names begining with an; are to be
found in all Sommersett, Dorsett, Glocester and the West
of Wiltshire, as there are 10 𝔚𝔦𝔩𝔩𝔰, so 14 𝔞𝔫𝔰, about
𝔖𝔱𝔬𝔫𝔞𝔤𝔢, the 𝔚𝔦𝔩𝔩𝔰 voting that it was a Temple, the
𝔞𝔫𝔰 that it was a Temple of *Andraste,* alias *Anraith,*
alias *Andates.*

Q. But of what forme and countenance was this Idoll?
Gildas sapiens (alias *Badonicus*) an old Briton,-borne at
Bathe about 20 miles from 𝔖𝔱𝔬𝔫𝔞𝔤𝔢 *Anno Domini* 493.
in his Book *de excidio Britannorum* describeth the Idols
of that his native Country in these words:

*Nec enumerans patriæ portenta ipsa diabolica, pene
numero Ægyptiaca vincentia, quorum nonnulla, lineamentis adhuc deformibus, intra vel extra deserta mœnia solito more rigentia, torvis vultibus intuemur.* He
1.   doth charactarize them, first by their monstrous shape,
implied in the word *portenta.*

2. by their Father and Patron, in *ipsa Diabolica.*

3. by their multitude, in *pene numero Ægyp iaca vincentia,* although they Goldified their very Leeks and
Onyons, to encrease their number, insomuch that Juve-
nal scoffed at them, saying, *felices gentes, quibus hæc
noscuntur,* etc.

4. by their deformed lineaments, *in lineamentis deformibus.*

5. by their Temples, in *intra vel extra mœnia.*

6. by their long standing in the word, *adhuc,* from
the begining of the world till his daies.

7. by their bullish countenances, in *torvis vultibus.*
For *torvus* comes from *Taurus.* Gold. Dictio. and as
these words of Gildas, so the bullish names of divers circumjacent parrishes, do intimate, that *Anraith* was a
very Bullegger, as 𝔅𝔲𝔩𝔣𝔬𝔯𝔡, two 𝔅𝔩𝔲𝔫𝔡𝔬𝔬𝔫𝔰, *orthog.* 𝔅𝔲𝔩-
lant-

lanſdownes, (i. e.) *Bulls-Temple Downes*, and Wⅿll=
fall, *orthog.* Bullfall, (i. e.) *Bul Devil*, and why might
not the old Britons have their *Bul Devil*, as well as the
Israelites their *Calf Devill*, and the Egyptians their *Ox
Devil, Apis?*

12. In this Temple the said Victors sacrificed their
Captives and Spoiles to their said Idoll of Victorie, where
I shall shew, that

1. The said Britons usually sacrificed their Captives
and Spoiles,

2. to *Andates*, aliàs *Anraith*, in Temples consecrated.

3. That they sacrificed their captives and spoiles there
in this Temple of *Andate*.

The Britons usually sacrificed their Captives and Spoiles
of war, according to the testimony of Julius Cæsar [1], when
he invaded this Island, *Qui in bello versantur, aut pro
victimis homines* [2] *immolant, aut se inmolaturos vovent,*
(i. e.) *They which addict themselves to warr either sacrifice, or vow they will sacrifice men,* (i. e.) *their Captives, as Victimes for Victory* (saith he). *The Majesty of the immortal* [3] *Goddess would not be pleased, un-
less they offer up the life of a Captive, or the life of a
man, and they have sacrificed or publickly instituted,
and some of them* (saith he) *make hallow images of vast
magnitude, with twiggs wreathed about together, whose
members they fill up with living men,* (i. e.) *Captives,
and so burn the Images, men and all together:* and these
[4] instanses are sufficient to prove, that the old Britons
did usually sacrifice their Captives.

---

[1] Cæsar's Com. I. lib. * 5ᵗᵒ. [* L. 6ᵗᵒ. *H.*]   [2] *Emolantur* MS.
H.   [3] F. *Gods.* H.   [4] Sic. *H.*

2. They

2. They usually sacrificed their Captives and spoiles to *Andates* in her Temple; and this I prove out of Cornelius Tacitus. The Romans having conquered Britaine, tyrannized so intollerably over them, that Prasutagus, King of the *Iceni*, that he might free his Subjects from their calamities, made the Romane Emperor Nero his Heir, hoping that he, and his, should thereby have the more favour, during his life at least; but the Romanes taking all for their owne, presently tyrannized infinitely the more, whipped his Queen Baodicea, ravished his daughters, and plundered his Subjects of all their estates, whereupon his wife Baodicea (whom Gildas termes the subtill Lioness) stirring up first the *Trinobantes* (i. e.) the *Londoners,* and afterwards the Britons in generall, raised a most blody warr against the Romans, cut off their two Colonies *Verolamium,* and *Camalodunum,* destroyed [1] three in the Legion, put Catus Decianus to flight, destroyed 80000 of them, some by the sword, and some by sacrificing them with the greatest crueltie to *Andates* in her Temple.

And that those old Britons sacrificed their Captives also to *Andates* in this her Temple, may appear by this, that it had all accomodations for such heathonish sacrifices, as an internall, or spatious, Court, lying round about, marked with the Letter *A* in the frontispice, wherein the Victimes for oblation were slain, into which it was unlawfull for any prophane person to enter. It was seperated from the circumjacent plain with a large trench, (marked with *B*) instead of a wall, as a boundarie about the Temple, most conformable to the maine

---

[1] F. *their ninth Legion.* H.

work

work, wholy exposed to open view. Without this Trench
the common promiscuous multitude, with zeal too much
attended their Idolatrous sacrifices, and might see the
oblations, but not come within them. *   *   *   *   *

*   *   *   *   *   *   *   *   *   *   *   *   *   *   *

*   *   *   *   *   *   *   *   *   *   *   *   *   *   *

Cætera desunt.
Vide Inigo Jones.

*Gay's signature has been
taken, for the 1986 edition, from
the 1669 insertions in Nettlecombe's parish
register. That year he recorded three
burials. They were the last
entries that he made.*

2.
Conjectures
on Stonehenge

| Easton's 1815 compilation

DESCRIPTION

OF

STONEHENGE.

JEFFERY OF MONMOUTH,

BISHOP OF ST. ASAPH.

Anno 1130.

STONEHENGE was a Monument erected in the reign of Aurelius Ambrosius, by Ambrose Merlin, to perpetuate the treachery of Hengist, the Saxon General; who, having desired a friendly meeting with Vortigern, at the Monastery of Ambresbury, assassinated him, with four hundred and sixty of his Barons and Consuls; after which the bodies of the slaughtered Britons were interred in a burying place near the Monastery where they had received their deaths; and Aurelius Ambrosius going to see the sepulchre soon after he had mounted the British throne, not only shed tears at the sight of it, but resolved to perpetuate the memory of that piece of ground which was honored with the bodies of so many noble patriots that died for their country, with some noble Monument.

In order to this, the King, after summoning together several carpenters and masons, commanded them to employ the utmost of their art in contriving

B

a proper structure; but they, out of diffidence of their own skill, refusing to undertake it, Merlin, who had been the prophet of Vortigern, was sent for to exercise his abilities; and he immediately advised Aurelius to send for the Giants' Dance in Killaraus, a mountain in Ireland: for there is, said he, a structure of Stones there, which none of this age could raise without a profound knowledge of the mechanical arts: they are Stones of a vast magnitude, and wonderful quality; and if they can be placed here as they stand there, they will remain for ever.

These Stones, continued Merlin, are mystical, and of a medicinal virtue. The Giants of old brought them from the farthest coasts of Africa, and placed them in Ireland, while they inhabited that country. Their design in this was to make baths in them, when they should be taken with any illness; for their method was to wash the Stones, and put their sick into the water, which infallibly cured them. With the like success they cured wounds also, adding only the application of some herbs; and there is not a Stone there, concluded Merlin, which has not some healing virtue.

Aurelius forthwith sent his brother Uther, attended with fifteen thousand young men, under the direction of Merlin, for these wonderful Stones: and at their arrival at the place where they stood, Merlin bade the men try their force, and see whether strength or art could do more towards taking them down. The command was no sooner given, than some of the young men who had prepared cables, others who had provided small ropes, and some who had furnished themselves with ladders for the work, applied those implements to the several parts of the building, and with one accord, the whole army attempted the removal of the Giants' Dance—but all to no purpose. Merlin, laughing at their vain efforts, then began his own contrivances: and when he had placed the engines in their proper order, which he thought necessary for the work, he took down the Stones with incredible facility, and withal gave directions for carrying them to Mount Ambre.

The Stones were no sooner brought to this mountain, than the King summoned to it the Bishops, the Abbots, and the people of all other orders and qualities, from every part of Britain, to celebrate with joy and honor, the setting them up.   And when the parties were all assembled, Aurelius with royal pomp, celebrated the feast of Pentecost, the solemnity whereof he continued the three following days. In the mean time, the King having bestowed all places of honor that were vacant on his domestics, as a reward for their good services, he next ordered Merlin to go to work upon the Monument, and rear up the Stones that were prepared for it about the Sepulchre of the slaughtered Britons; which he forthwith did in the same form as they stood in the mountain of Killaraus; and, as the British historian concludes, thereby gave a manifest proof of the prevalence of art above strength.

Tradition varies from history in the story touching the removal of this Monument from the mountain of Killaraus to that of Ambrius, and delivers it to this brief effect:

The prophet Merlin, desirous of having a parcel of Stones, which grew in an odd sort of form in a backside belonging to an old Woman in Ireland, transported from thence to Salisbury Plain, employed the Devil upon the work ; who, the night after, dressing himself like a gentleman, and taking a large bag of money in his hand, presented himself before the good Woman as she was sitting at her table, and acquainted her of the purchase he was come to

B 2

57

make; the Fiend, at the same time, pouring out his money on the board before her, and offering her as much for the Stones as she could reckon while he should be taking them away.

The money was all in odd sorts of coins, such as four-penny-half-penny pieces, nine-penny pieces, thirteen-penny-half-penny pieces, and the like; but, nevertheless, the Devil's proposals seemed so very advantageous, that, notwithstanding the difficulty there would be in reckoning the money, the old Woman could not avoid complying with it, as she imagined the removal of her Stones by a single man would be a work of almost infinite time, and that she should be able to tell as much money while it should be about, as would make her as rich as a Princess. But the bargain was no sooner made, and she had no sooner laid her fingers on a four-penny-half-penny coin, than the Devil, with an audible voice, cried out, " Hold!" and said, " The Stones are gone." The old Woman disregarding what he said, however, peeped out into her backside, and, to her great amazement, it was even so as Satan had spoken; for the common Deceiver of mankind in an instant took down the Stones, bound them up in a wyth, and conveyed them to Salisbury Plain. But, just before he got to Mount Ambre, the wyth slackened, and as he was crossing the river Avon at Bulford, one of the Stones dropped down into the water, where it lies to this very hour; the rest were immediately reared up on the spot of ground destined by Merlin for them: and the Devil, pleased with the accomplishment of his work, declared upon fixing the last stone, that nobody should be ever able to tell how the Fabric, or any of the parts of which it is composed, came there.

A Friar, who had lain all night concealed near the building, hearing the Devil's declaration, replied to it, by saying, " That is more than thee canst tell;" which put Satan into such a passion, that he snatched up a pillar, and hurled it at the Friar, with an intention to bruise him to dirt; but he running for his life, the stone, in its fall, only reached his heel, and struck him in it; the mark of which appears in that Pillar even unto this day, and is called *The Friar's Heel.*

———

GIRALDUS CAMBRENSIS says, " There was in Ireland, in ancient times, a pile of Stones worthy admiration, called *The Giants' Dance;* because Giants from the remotest parts of Africa brought them into Ireland; and in the plains of Kildare, not far from the castle of Naase, as well by force of art, as strength, miraculously set them up. These Stones, Aurelius Ambrosius, King of the Britons, procured Merlin by supernatural means to bring from Ireland into Britain. And that he might leave some famous Monument of so great a treason, to after ages, in the same order. and art as they stood formerly, set them up where the flower of the British nation fell by the cut-throat practice of the Saxons; and where, under pretence of peace, the ill-secured youth of the kingdom, by murderous designs, were slain.

B 3

CAMDEN.

Anno 1600.

TOWARDS the north, about six miles from Salisbury, in the plain, is to be seen an huge and monstrous piece of Work, such as Cicero termeth *insanam substructionem;* for, within the circuit of a ditch, there are erected in manner of a crown, in three ranks or courses, one within another, certain mighty and unrought Stones, whereof some are twenty-eight feet high, and seven broad; upon the heads of which, others, like overthwart pieces, do bear and rest crosswise, with a small tenon and mortise, so as the whole frame seemeth to hang; whereof we call it *Stonehenge*, like as our old historians termed it for the greatness, *Chorea Gigantum*, The Giants' Dance. Our countrymen reckon this for one of our wonders and miracles; and much they marvel from whence such huge stones were brought, considering that in all those quarters bordering thereupon, there is hardly to be found any common stones at all for building: as also by what means they were set up. For my own part, about these points, I am not curiously to argue and dispute, but rather to lament, with much grief, that the Authors of so notable a Monument are thus buried in oblivion. Yet some there are that think them to be no natural stones hewn out of the rock, but artificially made of pure sand: and by some gluey and unctious matter knit and incorporate together, like as those ancient trophies and monuments of victory which I have seen in Yorkshire. And what marvel? Read we not, I pray you, in Pliny, that the sand or dust of Puteoli, being covered over with water, becometh forthwith a very stone? That the cisterns in Rome, of sand digged out of the ground, and the strongest kind of lime, wrought together, grow so hard, that they seem stones indeed? And that statues and images of marble scalings, and small grit, grow together so compact and firm, that they are deemed entire and solid marble? The common saying is, that Ambrosius Aurelianus, or his brother Uther, did rear them up by the art of Merlin, &c.

North View of Stonehenge.

INIGO JONES,

ARCHITECT TO KING JAMES I.

Anno 1655.

———

Th is Antiquity, called by Henry Huntingdon, the second; by Polyolbion, first wonder of the land; because the architraves are set upon the heads of the upright stones, and hang, as it were, in the air, is generally known by the name of *Stone-Henge*. It is sited upon the Plain in the county of Wiltshire, in England, not far from Amesbury, the foundations of whose buildings, frequently digged up, render it to have been in times past, a town of no small fame, six miles at least from New Salisbury, northwards.

The whole Work in general being of a circular form, is one hundred and ten feet diameter, double winged about, without a roof, anciently environed with a deep trench, still appearing, about thirty feet broad; so that betwixt it and the Work itself, a large and void space of ground being left, it had from the Plain three open entrances, the most conspicuous thereof lying north-east; at each of which was raised. on the outside. of the trench aforesaid, two huge stones gatewise; parallel whereunto, on the inside, two others of less proportion. The inner part of the Work, consisting of an hexagonal figure, was raised by due symmetry, upon the bases of four equilateral triangles, which formed the whole structure. This inner part likewise was double, having, within also, another hexagon raised; and all that part within the trench, sited upon a commanding ground, eminent, and higher much than any of the Plain lying without; and in the midst thereof, upon the foundation of a hard chalk, the Work itself was placed: insomuch, that from whatever part soever they came into it, they rose by an easy ascending hill.

In the inmost part of the Work, there is a Stone, appearing not much above the surface of the earth, and lying towards the East, four feet broad, and sixteen feet long, which, whether it might be an *Altar* or no, I leave to the judgment of others; because so overwhelmed with the ruins of this work, that I could make no search after it, but even with much difficulty took the aforesaid proportions thereof: yet, for my part, I can apprehend no valid reasons to the contrary, except that the whole Constructure being circular in form, the Altar shewed rather to have been placed upon the centre of the circle, than inclined to the circumference. Nevertheless, it cannot be denied, but, being so fitted, the Cell (as I may call it) was thereby left more free, for the due performance of those several superstitious rites, which their idolatry led them to.

The great stones, which made the entrances from the outside of the trench, are seven feet broad, three feet thick, and twenty high.

The parallel stones, on he inside of the trench, are four feet broad and three feet thick; but they lie so broken, and ruined by time, that their proportion in height cannot be distinguished, much less exactly measured.

The stones which make the outer circle were seven feet in breadth, three feet and a half in thickness, and fifteen feet and a half in height; each stone having two tenons mortised into the architrave, continuing upon them throughout the whole circumference; for these architraves, being jointly directed in the middle of each of the perpendicular stones, that their weight might have an equal bearing; and upon each side of the joint, a tenon wrought (as yet remains to be seen), it may positively be concluded thereby, the architrave continued round about this outward circle.

The smaller stones of the inner circle are one foot and a half in breadth, one foot thick, and six feet high. These had no architraves upon them, but were raised perpendicular, of a pyramidal form. That there was no architrave upon these may be hence concluded, the stones being too small to carry such a weight, the spaces being also too wide to admit of an architrave upon them without danger of breaking; and being but six feet high, there could not possibly be a convenient head-height remaining for a passage underneath; especially, considering fully the greatness of the whole Work.

The stones of the greater hexagon are seven feet and a half in breadth, three feet nine inches in thickness, and twenty feet in height, each stone having one tenon in the middle.

The stones of the hexagon within are two feet six inches broad, one foot and a half thick, and eight feet high; in form pyramidal, like those of the inner circle.

The architrave, lying round about upon the upright stones of the outward circle, being mortised into them, and jointed in the middle of each of the perpendicular stones, is three feet and a half broad, and two feet and a half high.

The architrave, which lieth on the top of the great stones of the hexagon, and mortised also into them, is sixteen feet long, three feet nine inches broad, and three feet four inches high. This architrave, continuing only from stone to stone. left betwixt every two and two, a void space, free to the air, uncovered; for if they had been continued throughout the whole hexagon, then necessarily there must have been two tenons upon each of the said stones, as those of the outward circle had; but being disposed as aforesaid, that one which was in the middle, and yet remains apparent, was sufficient for the thing intended.

The stones of the greater hexagon, and outward circle, after so long contest with the violence of time, and injury of the weather, are, for the most part, standing at this day; which though not all at their full height, as when first set up, yet the footsteps, nevertheless, of many of them, as expressed in the design, are still remaining in their proper places. Those of the inner circle, and lesser hexagon, not only exposed to the fury of all devouring age, but to the rage of men likewise, have been more subject to ruin; for being of no extraordinary proportions, they might easily be beaten down, or digged up, and at pleasure made use of for other occasions; which I am the rather induced to believe, because since my first measuring the work, not one fragment of some of them then standing, is now to be found.

I conceive Stonehenge to have been erected after the Tuscan order of architecture, and open to the heavens, and dedicated to the God Cœlus, by some authors called Cœlum, by others Uranus, from whom the ancients imagined all things took their beginning. My reasons are, first, with respect to the situation thereof; for it stands in a plain, remote from any town or village, in a free and open air, without any groves or woods about it. Secondly, in regard of the aspect; for Stonehenge was never covered, but built without a roof: which decorum the Romans ever observed, both in the situation and aspect of the temples dedicated to this their God, and to Jove the Lightner, the Sun, and the Moon. Another reason I find also why they built their temples to Cœlus, and those other deities, uncovered, as Stonehenge; because they counted it an heinous matter to see those Gods confined under a roof, whose doing good consisted in being abroad.

DR. CHARLTON,

PHYSICIAN TO KING CHARLES II.

Anno 1660.

I ADVENTURE to acquaint you with my conjecture, concerning the time when Stonehenge was first set up, which I take to be in the beginning of the reign of that excellent Prince, Alfred, or Allured; who, as he was the first anointed King of this island, so was he the first learned King, and most munificent patron of scholars, that ever swayed the sceptre of Britain; for all our chronicles agreeingly deliver that he was scarcely seated in his throne, when there came over greater swarms of Danes than ever before, to infest his dominions; and that, after many unfortunate battles with them, he was reduced to that extremity, that leaving his large monarchy to the rage and rapine of those insulting Pagans, he fled, for safety of his life, into the marshes of Somersetshire, where, for two years, he lay concealed in a poor disguise, sustaining himself by fishing and fowling. Among other adventures that befel this glorious person in this dark eclipse, it is not unworthy remembrance, that on a time, as he was sitting in the chimney corner, in the cottage of a Cow-herd (who entertained him in his service), and busied in trimming his bow and arrows, a cake of dough, lying to be baked on the hearth before him, chanced to be burned; which the good wife imputing to his neglect, in great fury cast away his bow and arrows, and sharply checking him, said, " Thou fellow, dost thou see the bread burn before thy face, and wilt not turn it? and yet thou art glad to eat it before it be half baked." Shortly after this, learning policy from adversity, and deriving courage from necessity, he ventured in the habit of a common minstrel, to enter the Danes' camp (in Wiltshire), and probably not far from the place where Stonehenge stands), and having viewed the manner of their encamping, and observed their security, he returned back to several of his Lords, retreated into the island called Edlinsey, environed with two rivers, Thane and Parret, in Somersetshire, and acquainted them in how careless, and open a posture he found the enemy; re-collected the scattered remains of his forces, and with these, surprising the Danes, and putting them first into a panic terror, and then to flight, gave them so considerable a defeat, that they immediately submitted to a treaty, and delivered hostages for performance of conditions.

Now, considering the extreme low ebb of fortune to which this excellent King was at that time brought, and the high flood of prosperity that had in the mean while advanced the Danes over all parts of his dominions, insomuch that nothing seemed wanting to complete their conquest, but only to find out the few defendants who remained in obscurity; and withal reflecting on that former-mentioned custom of that ambitious and martial nation, to erect Courts Royal of huge stones, according to the manner described, for the election of their Kings, in all countries where the happy success of their arms had given them a title to sovereignty; I am apt to believe that, having then overrun the whole kingdom, except only Somersetshire, and encamping their main army in Wiltshire, for near upon two years together; and setting up their rest in a confidence to perpetuate their newly acquired power, they employed themselves during that time of leisure and jollity in erecting Stonehenge, as a

c

place wherein to elect and inaugurate their supreme commander, King of England; the weakness of the distressed Alfred affording them a fit opportunity, and that country yielding them fit materials for so great and stupendous a work. Nor is it improbable, that the great supinity and disorder in which the Royal Spy found them, when the magic of his fiddle had charmed them into an imperception of the majesty of his person, and procured him a free welcome into their camp, might be occasioned by the jubilee they celebrated, after they had finished their laborious task, and therein newly crowned their King, after a triumphal manner, such as at once corresponded with the fashion of their ancestors, and expressed the profuseness of their public joy. For many of our historians relate, that the Danish army was at that time let loose to luxury and revelling; and that the unknown Musician was brought to play before their King, Gurmund, in his tent, during a long magnificent feast. But perhaps I may be thought too bold in daring from such slender passages and circumstantial hints, thus precisely to guess at the age of this antiquity; concerning whose origin, neither history nor tradition, hath left any glimpse of light whereby the inquisitive might be guided through the darksome vale of uncertainty to the delightful mansions of truth. Leaving every man therefore, to the liberty of his own thoughts touching this particular; as also whatever else hath been said of the Monument itself, and its original designation; I here put a period to this discourse; wherein, though I have ventured to contend with oblivion, I had no design to usurp upon the judgment of others.

At this point in Easton's work is an
abridged version of *A Fool's Bolt son* (sic)
shoot (sic) *at Stonage* which is omitted
from here as it has already been printed
in full. The work is credited to John
Gibbons and dated to about 1660, with
a note that it was "collected by Hearne,
the Antiquarian; and printed in Peter
Langtoft's Chronicle"

GIBSON.

FROM CAMDEN'S BRITANNIA.

ABOUT seven miles north of Salisbury, is Stonehenge; a piece of antiquity so famous, as to have
gained the admiration of all ages, and engaged the
pens of some very considerable Authors. It is of
itself so singular, and receives so little light from
history, that almost every one has advanced a new
notion. To give the several conjectures, with some
short remarks, is as much as the narrow compass of
our design will allow. But not to hunt after such
uncertainties, and in the mean time to pass over
what lies before our eyes, we will premise a description of the place as it now stands, much more distinct than what Mr. Camden has left us. It is situated on a rising ground, environed with a deep
trench, still appearing, and about thirty feet broad.
From the plain it has had three entrances, the most
considerable lying north-east; at each of which was
raised, on the outside of the trench, two huge stones
gatewise; parallel whereunto, on the inside, were
two others of less proportion. After one has passed
this ditch, he ascends thirty five yards before he
comes at the work itself; which consists of four
circles of stones The outward circle is about one
hundred feet diameter; the stones whereof are very
large, four yards in height, two in breadth, and one
in thickness. Two yards and a half within this great
circle, is a range of lesser stones. Three yards farther is the principal part of the work, called by Mr.
Jones, the Cell, of an irregular figure, made up of
two rows of stones; the outer of which consists of
great upright stones, in height twenty feet, in breadth
two yards, and in thickness one yard. These are
coupled at the top by large transome stones like

architraves, which are seven feet long, and about three and a half thick. Within this, was also another range of lesser pyramidal stones, of about six feet in height. In the inmost part of the Cell Mr. Jones observed a stone, appearing not above the surface of the earth, and lying toward the east, four feet broad, and sixteen long; which he called the Altar Stone.

And so much for the structure and dimensions of the Monument; only it may in general be observed, That the stones are not artificial, as Mr. Camden, and some others would persuade us, but purely natural, as Mr. Jones has asserted.

The opinions about it may be reduced to these seven heads:

1. That it is a work of the Phœnicians, as Mr. Sammes in his *Britannia* conceits; a conjecture that hath met with so little approbation, that I shall not stay to confute it.

2. That it was a Temple of the Druids long before the coming in of the Romans, which Mr. John Aubrey, Fellow of the Royal Society, endeavours to prove in his manuscript treatise entitled *Monumenta Britannica.*

3. That it was an old Triumphal British Monument, erected to Anaraith, the goddess of victory, after a bloody battle won by the illustrious Stannings and his Cangick giants, from Divitiacus and his Belgæ; and that the captives and spoils were sacrificed to the said idol in this temple: an opinion advanced (upon what grounds I know not) in an anonymous M.S. written about the year 1666, and now in the hands of the learned Mr. Andrew Paschal, rector of Chedzoy, near Bridgwater.

4. That it was a Monument raised by the Britons

in memory of Queen Boadicea; advanced by the Author of *Nero Cæsar*.

5 That it was a Temple built by the Romans to the God Cœlum, or Terminus, of the Tuscan order, is Mr. Jones's opinion in his ingenious conjecture upon this subject.

6 That it was the Burying Place of Uther, Pendragon, Constantine, Ambrosius, and other British Kings; or, as others would have it, a Monument erected by Ambrosius in memory of the Britons here slain.

7. That it was a Danish Monument erected either for a burial place, a trophy for some victory, or a place for election, or coronation, of their kings.

These are all the opinions which have been advanced about it. And in general, I should think, one need make no scruple to affirm, that it is a British Monument; since it does not appear that any other nation had so much footing in this kingdom, as to be authors of such a rude and magnificent pile. For, to pass by the Phœnicians: that it could not be built by the Romans, is evident from the rudeness of the whole work. So that (as Mr. Aubrey has very well observed), whilst Mr. Jones pleases himself with retrieving a piece of architecture out of Vitruvius, he abuses his Reader by a false scheme of the whole work. For the cell is not of an exact hexagonal figure, but very irregular, and comes nearer a heptagon; so that the whole work cannot be formed upon the basis of four equilateral triangles, as Mr. Jones supposed; neither are the entrances into the trench so regular, and so equidistant, as that author would make them. Till these, and some other doubts (which may be raised from the order of the building) be resolved, and till we are assured from good authority that the Romans used to build such stupendous piles, six or seven miles from any of their stations, without any inscription or Roman coin ever found near them, it cannot be safe to close with Mr. Jones; though his book be otherwise a learned and ingenious piece.

Nor could it be built by the Danes; as for many other reasons, so particularly, because it is mentioned in some manuscripts of Ninius; who, as every body knows, wrote almost two hundred years before the Danes were masters of any considerable part of this island.

One great argument by which Mr. Jones established his own opinion, is, that it is a thing altogether improbable the Britons could build such a monument. But the contrary is evident from the fortifications of Caractacus's camp; from the vast stones mentioned by Dr. Plott, to be in or near the British city or fortification, by Wrottesly, in Staffordshire; and from the parcel of stones (not unlike Stonehenge) that are in some parts of Scotland and Wales; whither the Romans and Danes never came. 'Tis true, those monuments have not their architraves (which Stonehenge has, not only in the stones round the cell, but also on the great stones of the utmost circle); and this makes it probable, that Stonehenge was built after the Romans came in, and in imitation of some of their structures; though, as to the general part of the work, it appears to have been inartificial, and favours of their primitive rudeness; for, that the Britons, among other parts of humanity, and neat living, learnt something of architecture from the Romans, is plain, from the Life of Agricola.

In that other point, the occasion upon which it was built, it is easier to confute those opinions that have already appeared, than to deliver a true one.

D

There is no authority to convince a man of the truth of what Nero Cæsar, or Mr. Paschal's M. S. have laid down; and it is hard to assent to the later British writers, who tell us it was the sepulchre of the British kings; or else in memory of the Britons here massacred by the Saxons. For, not to mention the improbability of what those authors have delivered, they tell us farther, that the Kings buried, or Britons martyred, in this place, were Christians. Now it is strange, if so, there should be no cross, nor any other token of the British faith upon this monument. What reason can be given why the surviving friends of these princes and noblemen, should not be as careful of their memory, as they of the same age were of King Arthur's, in whose monument at Glassenbury was found so distinct an inscription? But what makes more against this opinion, are the ashes and pieces of burnt bones, here frequently found; by which it is plain it was no Christian burial place; since sacrifices, and the custom of burning the dead, grew out of use, upon the receiving of the Christian faith.

For the name, Leland's opinion, that the British one, *Choir Gaure*, should not be translated *Chorea Gigantum*, but *Chorea nobilis;* or else that *Gaure* is put for *Vaure*, which makes it *Chorea Magna;* is probable enough. But the true Saxon name seems to be Stanhengist (and so it is writ in the *Monasticon*, out of a manuscript of good authority), from the memorable slaughter which Hengist, the Saxon, here made of the Britons. For though it is not very probable that they were erected by Ambrosius in memory of the Britons, yet without doubt, that treacherous slaughter was committed at or near this place. If this etymology may be allowed, that which received derivation from the hanging of stones, may be as far from the truth, as that of the vulgar *Stone-edge*, from stones set on edge.

DR. STUKELEY

Anno 1743.

STONEHENGE stands, not upon the summit of a hill, but pretty near it; and, for more than three quarters of the circuit you ascend to it very gently from the lower ground: at half a mile distance the appearance of it is stately, awful, and really august. As you advance nearer, especially up the avenue (which is now most perfect), the greatness of its contour fills the eye in an astonishing manner.

Stonehenge is inclosed within a circular ditch: after one has passed this ditch, he ascends thirty-five yards before he comes at the work itself. This measure is the same as that which Webb calls one hundred and ten feet, the diameter of the work; for the area inclosed by a ditch, wherein Stonehenge is situate, is in diameter three times the diameter of Stonehenge: therefore, the distance between the verge of the ditch within side, quite round to the work of the Temple, is equal to the diameter of the Temple.*

When you enter the building, whether on foot or horseback, and cast your eyes around upon the yawning ruins, you are struck into an extatic reverie, which none can describe, and they only can be

* The Reader is to observe, that Dr. Stukeley's measure of this Temple, is by the Hebrew, Phœnician, or Egyptian cubit, which, compared to the English foot, amounts to twenty inches and four fifths.

D 2

sensible of, that feel it. Other buildings fall by
piece-meal: but here a single stone is a ruin, and
lies like the haughty carcase of Goliah. Yet there
is as much of it undemolished, as enables us sufficiently to recover its form, when it was in its most
perfect state. When we advance farther, the dark
part of the ponderous imposts over our heads, the
chasm of sky between the jambs of the cell, the odd
construction of the whole, and the greatness of every
part, surprises. We may well cry out in the Poet's
words, *tantum religio potuit.*

If you look upon the perfect part, you fancy entire quarries mounted up into the air: if upon the
rude havock below, you see as it were the bowels of
a mountain turned inside outwards. Directly down
the avenue, to the north-east, the apex of an hill
terminates the horizon; between which, and the
bottom of a valley, you see the Cursus, a work
which has never yet been taken notice of; being a
space of ground, included between two long banks,
going parallel east and west, at three hundred and
fifty feet distance; the length ten thousand feet:
this was designed for the horse races and games, like
the Olympic, the Isthmian, &c. of the Greeks. In
the valley, on this side of it, the strait part of the
avenue terminates in two branches; that on the left
hand leads to the Cursus; that, on the right, directly up the hill, between two famous groups of
barrows, each consisting of seven in number; the
farthest, or those northward, I call *The Oldest Kings'
Barrows;* the hithermost are vulgarly called *The
Seven Kings' Graves.**

Many, from the great quantity of these sepulchral

---

* These seven last are now inclosed and planted with Scotch
firs, by his Grace the Duke of Queensberry, since the Doctor's
time, and have a delightful prospect from Stonehenge.

tumuli here, injudiciously conclude, that there have been great battles upon the plain; and that the slain were buried there; but they are really no other than family burying places, set near this Temple, for the same reason as we bury in church-yards, and consecrated ground.

Of the outer circle of Stonehenge, which, in its perfection consisted of sixty stones, thirty uprights, and thirty imposts, there are more than half the uprights, *viz.* seventeen, left standing.

Eleven of these uprights remain contiguous by the grand entrance, with five imposts upon them. One upright, at the back of the Temple, or on the south-west, leans upon a stone of the inner circle. There are six more lying, upon the ground, whole, or in pieces; so that twenty-four out of thirty, are still visible at the place. There is but one impost more in its proper place, and but two lying upon the ground; so that twenty-two are carried off. Somewhat more than eight feet inward, from the inside of this exterior circle, is another circle of much lesser stones. The stones that compose it are forty in number, forming with the outer circle (as it were) a circular portico: a most beautiful walk, and of a pretty effect.

Of these greater stones of the Adytum, as I observed before, there are none wanting. They are all on the spot; ten upright stones; five cornishes. The trilithon first, on the left hand, is entire in situ, but vastly decayed, especially the cornish. There are such deep holes corroded in some places, that daws make their nests in them. The next trilithon, on the left hand, is entire, composed of three most beautiful stones. The cornish happened to be of a very durable kind of English marble, and has not been much impaired by weather. My Lord Winchelsea and myself took a considerable walk on the top of it; but it was a frightful situation. The trilithon of the upper end of the adytum was an extraordinary beauty: but alas! through the indiscretion, probably, of somebody digging there, between them and the altar, the noble impost is dislodged from its airy seat, and fallen upon the altar; where its huge bulk lies unfractured. The two uprights that supported it are the most delicate stones of the whole work. They were, I believe, above thirty feet long, and well chizelled, finely tapered, and proportioned in their dimensions. That southward is broke in two, lying upon the altar. The other stands entire, but leans upon one of the stones of the inner oval. The root end, or unhewn part, of both, are raised somewhat above ground. We cannot be sure of the true height of this when it was perfect; but I am sure, fifteen cubits, which I have assigned, is the lowest. The next trilithon, that toward the west, is entire; except, that some of the end of the impost is fallen clean off; and all the upper edge diminished by time. The last trilithon, that on the right hand of the entrance into the adytum, has suffered much. The outer upright, being the jamb of the entrance, is still standing: the other upright and impost are both fallen forwards into the adytum, and broke each into three pieces; I suppose from digging near it.

Stonehenge is composed of two circles, and two ovals, respectively concentric. At the distance of two cubits inward from the greater oval, is described another lesser oval, on which the stones of the inner oval are to stand; nineteen stones in number, at about the central distance of three cubits. Their height is likewise unequal, as the trilithons, for they rise in height, as nearer the upper end of the adytum. From the ruins of those left, we may well suppose, the first next the entrance, and lowest, were four cubits high; the most advanced height behind the altar, might be five cubits, and perhaps more. The stones are somewhat of a pyramidal form, for they taper a little upward. They are of a much harder sort than the other stones of the lesser circle. They were brought somewhere from the west. Of these there are only six remaining upright. The stumps of two are left on the south side by the altar; one or two were thrown down, probably by the fall of the upright of the first trilithon on the right hand. A stump of another remains by the upright there, still standing. Their exact measures, as to height, breadth, or thickness, cannot well be ascertained, for they took such as they could find best suiting their scantlings; but the stones were better shaped, and taller, as advancing towards the upper end of the cell.

The great oval consists of ten uprights; the inner, with the altar, of twenty; the great circle of thirty; the inner of forty. Ten, twenty, thirty, and forty together, make one hundred upright stones. Five imposts of the great oval, thirty of the great circle, the two stones standing on the back of the area, the stone lying within the entrance of the area, and that standing without. There seems to have been another stone lying upon the ground, by the vallum of the court, directly opposite the entrance of the avenue. All added together make just one hundred and forty stones; the number of which Stonehenge, a whole temple, is composed. Behold the solution of the mighty problem: the magical spell is broke, which has so long perplexed the vulgar! They think it is an ominous thing to count the true number of the stones; and whoever does so, shall certainly die after it. Thus the Druids contented themselves to live in huts and caves, whilst they employed many thousands of men, a whole country, to labor at these public structures, dedicated to the Deity.

The altar here is laid towards the upper end of

the adytum, at present flat on the ground, and squeezed (as it were) into it, by the weight of the ruins upon it: it is a kind of blue coarse marble, such as comes from Derbyshire. This altar is placed a little above the focus of the upper end of the ellipsis. Mr. Webb says it is four feet broad, sixteen long. Four feet is two cubits, two palms, which at four times, measures six feet. I believe its breadth is two cubits, three palms; *i. e.* one and an half: and that its first intended length was ten cubits, equal to the breadth of the trilithon before which it lies. But it is very difficult to come at its true length. 'Tis just a cubit thick, and has been squared. It lies between two centres, that of the compasses, and that of the string; leaving a convenient place quite round it, no doubt, as much as was necessary for their ministration.

Of the court, round the temple of Stonehenge, somewhat is already said, and of the two stones standing within the vallum: and of the two remarkable cavities, which have some correspondency therewith. I supposed they were places where two great vases of water stood for the service of the Temple, when they performed religious rites here. Sixty cubits is the diameter of Stonehenge: sixty more reaches the inner edge of the circular ditch of the court. The ditch was originally near thirty cubits broad; but through a long tract of time, and the infinity of coaches, horses, &c. coming every day to see the place, it is levelled very much. The entire diameter of the court, reaching to the outward verge of the ditch, is four times sixty cubits; which is about four hundred and ten feet. The five outer circles of the ditch are struck with a radius, of eighty, ninety, one hundred, one hundred and ten, and one hundred and twenty cubits. Just upon the inner verge of the ditch, at the entrance from the avenue, lies a very large stone, at present flat on the ground. The two stones within the vallum are very small stones, and ever were ten : the one stands, the other leans a little, probably from some idle people digging about it.

This stone, at the entrance, is a very great one, near as big as any one of the whole work ; and seems too, as little altered from its original form ; only thrown down, perhaps, by the like foolish curiosity of digging near it. It is near seven feet broad, and twenty feet long. If it stood originally, and a little leaning, it was one of those stones which the Welch call *crwm lecheu,* or bowing stones. There is, doubtless, crwm lecheu still standing in its original posture, and place in the avenue. It is much of the same dimensions as the other, though not so shapely; and stands in like manner, on the left hand, or south, of the middle line, of the length of the avenue. I surmise, the Druids considered the propriety of making the other a little more shapely than this; because within the area, and nearer the sacred fabric, there is the distance of one hundred and nineteen feet between them : to speak properly, eighty cubits. This stone has a hole in it, which is observable of like stones set thus near our like temples; the stone is twenty-four feet in circumference, sixteen above ground, nine broad, six thick. The use of it I cannot certainly tell ; but I am inclined to think, that as part of the religious worship in old patriarchal times, consisted in a solemn adoration, or three silent bowings; the first bowing might be performed at this stone, just without the ditch ; the second, perhaps, at the next stone, just within the ditch. They then turned by that stone, to the left hand, as the manner was in a procession round the Temple, both the priests and animals for sacrifice. At those two stones and water-vases, probably there was some washings, lustrations, or sprinklings, with holy water and other ceremonies, which I do not pretend to ascertain. Then upon the entry into the Temple, per-

haps they made their third bow, as in presence of
the Deity: after this, in the court, we may suppose
the Priests prepared the hecatombs, as customary
sacrifices. If that great stone just within the ditch,
always lay as it does now, flat on the ground, and
in situ (which I am not unwilling to believe), then,
I apprehend, it was a table for dressing the victims.

Thus have we finished the work, or principal
part, of this celebrated Wonder; properly the Temple, or Sacred Structure, as it may be called;
though its loftiest crest be composed of one stone
laid upon another.

The Cursus, about half a mile north of Stonehenge, across the valley, is the Cursus or Hippodrom
which I discovered August 6, 1723. It is a noble
monument of antiquity, and illustrates very much
the preceding account of Stonehenge. It was the
universal custom to celebrate games, feasts, exer-
cises, and sports at their most public and solemn
meetings to sacrifice; which was done quarterly
and anniversarily, at certain stated seasons of the
year. This great work is included between two
ditches, running east and west, in a parallel which
are three hundred and fifty feet asunder. When I
mention three hundred and fifty feet, I speak in the
gross, as we should set it down in an English scale.
This Cursus is a little above ten thousand feet long;
that is, it is made of six thousand Druid cubits in
length: a most noble work, contrived to reach from
the highest ground of two hills extended the inter-
mediate distance, over a gentle valley: so that the
whole Cursus lies immediately under the eye of the
most numerous quantity of spectators. To render
this the more convenient for sight, it is projected on
the side of a rising ground, chiefly looking southward towards Stonehenge. A delightful prospect
from the Temple, when this vast plain was crowded
with chariots, horsemen, and foot, attending these

solemnities, with innumerable multitudes! This Cursus, which is two miles long, has two entrances (as it were), gaps being left in two little ditches; and these gaps, which are opposite to each other, in the two ditches, are opposite to the straight part of the Stonehenge avenue.

I mentioned before, that at the bottom of the strait part of Stonehenge avenue, in the valley, the avenue divides itself into two parts; one goes directly east, towards Radsin; the other goes north-westward, and enters our Cursus nearly at the same distance west from the gaps, or entrances before-mentioned; as these gaps are from the east end of the Hippodrom. These gaps being at a convenient distance from that east end, may be thought to be in the nature of distance posts. It seems to me, that the turf of the adjacent ground, on both sides, has been originally taken off, and laid on the whole length of this Cursus; because it appears somewhat higher in level. Though this was an incredible labor, yet a fine design for the purpose of running. The earth of the vallum is likewise thrown inward. The east end of the Cursus is composed of a huge body of earth, a bank or long barrow, thrown up nearly the whole breadth of the Cursus. This seems to be the plain of session for the Judges of the prizes, and chief of the spectators. The west end of the Cursus is curved into an arch, like the end of the Roman Cursus; and there probably the chariots ran round in order to turn again: and there is an obscure barrow or two, round which they returned, as it were a meta.

This is the finest piece of ground that can be imagined for the purpose of a horse-race. The whole is commanded by the eye of a spectator in any part. In the middle is a valley, and pretty steep at present; yet only so, as that a British charioteer may have a good opportunity of shewing

that dexterity spoken of by Cæsar: but the exquisite softness of the turf prevents any great damage
by a fall. The ground of it hereabout declines
somewhat northward. The main part of this Hippodrom is upon a gentle ridge, running east and
west: this rendered the place cooler.

On the southern ridge, toward the west end of it,
are many considerable barrows; but none toward
the east end, for that would obstruct the view of
Stonehenge. There are many barrows, but of no
considerable bulk, on the north side, upon the extensive ascent, towards the great north long barrow.
This magnificent work of the Cursus is drawn due
east and west, except a small variation of four or
five degrees southward from the east. If we measure along the bank from the eastern meta, at seven
hundred cubits exactly, we come over against the
middle line of the strait part of the avenue to Stonehenge: five hundred cubits farther conducts us to
the gaps, or opposite entrances, I before mentioned;
which we suppose as distance posts. The whole
interval, between the eastern meta and these gaps,
is one thousand two hundred cubits. At one thousand cubits more we come to the place where the
west wing of the avenue enters the southern ditch
of the Cursus. That west wing, too, is just one
thousand cubits long to its union with the strait part
of Stonehenge avenue. Likewise the strait part of
Stonehenge avenue is just one thousand cubits long,
as mentioned in its proper place. This west wing
begins in the bottom of that valley which crosses
the middle of the Cursus; and sweeping along by
the bottom of the hill, in a gentle curve, meets with
the lower end of the strait part of Stonehenge
avenue, where the wing, or avenue, unites to it with
an equal angle. So that the whole work is laid out
with great judgment and symmetry, and curiously
adapted to the ground; which was well considered
before the plot was marked out by the first sur-

veyors. From the bottom of the valley, crossing the middle of the Cursus, to the western meta, is three thousand eight hundred cubits more; making in the whole six thousand cubits. The north end of the eastern meta does not extend so far as the northern bank of the Cursus: I suppose the reason is, that there might be liberty that way to stop the horses at the end of the course. Therefore they set out on the south side of the Cursus, and returned on the north side. I observe the ditch and bank towards the eastern end of the Cursus much obscured by the trampling of men and horses frequenting the spectacles here; this being the most thronged.

The Cursus is directly north from Stonehenge; so exactly, that the meridian line of Stonehenge passes precisely through the middle of the Cursus. And when we stand in the grand entrance of Stonehenge, and observe the two extremities of the Cursus, the eastern and western meta, they are exactly sixty degrees from the meridian line on each hand, making a third part of the circle of the horizon, by which we see the Druids well understood the geometry of a circle, and its measure of three hundred and sixty parts.

THE BARROWS.

I come now in the next place to speak of the Barrows, observable in great numbers round Stonehenge. We may very readily count fifty at a time in sight, round the place, easily distinguishable; but especially in the evening, when the sloping rays of the sun shine on the ground beyond them. These Barrows are the artificial ornaments of this vast and open plain. And it is no small entertainment for a curious person to remark their beauties, their variety in form and magnitude, their situation, &c. They are generally of a very elegant companiform

E

shape, and done with great nicety. There is like
wise a great variety in their shape and turn, and in
their diameters, and in their manner of composition.
In general they are always upon elevated ground,
in sight of the temple of Stonehenge; for they all
regard it. This shews they are but superficial
inspectors of things that fancy from hence great
battles on the plain; and that these are the tumul-
tuary burials of the slain. Quite otherwise: they
are assuredly the single sepulchres of Kings and
great personages, buried during a considerable space
of time; and that in peace. There are many groups
of them together, and as family burial places. The
variety of them seems to indicate some note of difference in the persons there interred, well known in
those ages. Probably the priests and laity were
some way distinguished; as well as different orders
and stations in them. Most of the barrows have
little ditches round extremely well defined. In
many is a circular ditch sixty cubits diameter, with
a very small tumulus in the centre: sixty, or even
one hundred cubits, is a very common diameter in
the large barrows.

In 1722, Lord Pembroke opened a Barrow in
order to find the position of the body observed in
those early days. He pitched upon one of those
south of Stonehenge, close upon the road thither
from Wilton, and on the east side of the road. It
is one of the double barrows, or where two are
inclosed in one ditch; one of these, which I suppose
the latter kind, and of a fine-turned bell fashion.
On the west side he made a section from the top to
the bottom; an entire segment from centre to circumference. The manner of composition of the
barrow was good earth quite through, except a coat
of chalk about two feet in thickness, covering it
quite over under the turf. Hence it appears that
the method of making these barrows was, to dig up
the turf for a space round, till the barrow was

brought to its intended bulk ; then with chalk dug out of the environing ditch, they powdered it all over. At the top, or centre of this barrow, not above three feet under the surface, my Lord found the skeleton of the interred, quite perfect, of a reasonable size, the head lying towards Stonehenge, northward.

The year following I begun upon a barrow north of Stonehenge, in that group south of the Cursus. It is one of the double barrows there, and the more easterly and lower of the two ; likewise somewhat less. It was reasonable to believe this was the sepulchre of a man and his wife ; and that the lesser was a daughter : and so it proved ; at least a female. We made a large cut on the top, from east to west. After the turf was taken off, we came to the layer of chalk, as before; then fine garden mould. About three feet below the surface, a layer of flints humouring the convexity of the barrow. This being about a foot thick, rested on a layer of soft mould, another foot, in which was inclosed an urn full of bones. This urn was of unbaked clay, of a dark reddish colour, and crumbled into pieces : it had been rudely wrought with small mouldings round the verge, and other circular channels on the outside, with several indentures between, made with a pointed tool. It appears to have been a girl of about fourteen years old by their bulk, and a great quantity of female ornaments mixed with the bones : all of which we gathered. Beads of all sorts, in great numbers; of glass of divers colours, most yellow, one black, many single, many in long pieces notched between, so as to resemble a string of beads, and these were generally of a blue colour. There were many of amber, of all shapes and sizes, flat squares, long squares, round, oblong, little and great. Likewise many of earth, of different shapes, magnitude, and colour ; some little and white, many large and flattish, like a button; others like a pully ; but all

E 2

had holes to run a string through, either through their diameter or sides. Many of the button sort seem to have been covered with metal, there being a rim worked in them, wherein to turn the edge of the covering. One of these was covered with a thin film of pure gold. These were the young lady's ornaments, and had all undergone the fire; so that what would easily consume fell to pieces as soon as handled. Much of the amber burnt half through. This person was a heroine; for we found the head of her javeline in brass: at bottom were two holes for the pin that fastened it to the staff: besides, there was a sharp bodkin round at one end, square at the other, where it went into the handle. I still preserve whatever is permanent in these trinkets. In the next barrow, at fourteen inches deep, we came to the entire skeleton of a man, the skull and all the bones exceeding rotten and perished through length of time. The body lay north and south; the head to the north.

We dug up one of those I call *Druids' Barrows*, a small tump, inclosed in a large circular ditch. I chose that next to Bush-Barrow, westward of it: Stonehenge bears hence north-east. We made a cross section, ten feet each way, three feet broad over its centre upon the cardinal points. At length we found a squarish hole cut into the solid chalk in the centre of the tumulus. It was three feet and a half; i. e. two cubits long, and near two feet broad; i. e. one cubit pointing directly to Stonehenge. It was one cubit and a half deep from the surface. In this little grave we found all the burnt bones of a man, but no signs of an urn. In some other barrows I opened were found large burnt bones of horses and dogs, along with human. Also of other animals, as seemed of fowls, hares, boars, deer, goats, or the like. Lord Pembroke told me of a brass sword dug up in a barrow here, which was sent to Oxford. In that very old barrow, near

Little Ambresbury, was found a very large brass weapon of twenty pounds weight, like a poleax, said to be given to Colonel Wyndham. In the great long barrow, farthest north from Stonehenge, which I call *North Long Barrow*, and supposed to be an Arcudruid's, was found one of those brass instruments, called celts, thirteen inches long, which I hold to belong to the Druids, wherewith they cut off the misleto. It is now in Sir Hans Sloane's cabinet.

West View of Stonehenge.

z 3

WOOD.

Anno 1747.

THE grand and only access to this Work is by ascending ground from the east, north-east, or rather from a point a small matter more to the north, which makes the building appear really majestic to such as approach it in front, and cannot fail of striking the person who considers it as a sacred structure, with religious awe. The line of two detached stones before the front of the fabric, directs to the middle of the most entire part of the body of the building; and this part consists of four great pillars, sustaining three large blocks of stone.

After passing the middle aperture of this tetrastyle frontispiece, a few paces bring us to the greatest wonder of the whole work; and that is, a block of stone of about fifteen feet and a half in length, lying edgewise on a flat stone, almost sunk into the ground, and so exactly counterpoised as to be put in motion by the force of a man's hand. This Rocking Stone appears to be something beyond the centre of the work; and the clear area in which we see it, and the stone whereon it rests, is most apparently surrounded with the remains of two double rows, or curved lines of pillars, some of which are standing, some are leaning against others, and some lie flat on the ground.

The outward line of pillars, in the body of the work, considered as the periphery of a circle, was manifestly composed, or intended to be composed, of thirty in number; for those that still remain answer such a division : and the second line of pillars, considered also as the periphery of a circle, concentric with the first line, seems to have been composed of nine and twenty in number; since the pillars now remaining in it answer that division, and no other, as I could find by innumerable trials : the third line of pillars, considered partly as the periphery of a circle, and partly as a right line, was composed of ten in number: and the inner line of pillars, considered also partly as a periphery of a circle, and partly as a right line, concentric with the former, seems to have been composed of nineteen in number, since the pillars in it answer that very division.

The altitude of the pillars in this fourth row seems to have been just half the altitude of the pillars behind them ; and the pillars of the second row seem to have risen just half as high as the pillars of the first row.

I have many reasons to believe that the same intercolumniation was intended, generally, in the second row of pillars, in respect to the breadth of those pillars, and the breadth of the voids between them, as appears to have been executed in the first row; and that the smaller pillars of the whole fabric were made of different breadths, thicknesses, and even shapes, according as the things varied from each other, which those pillars were intended to point out.

Stonehenge, whether considered in its ruins, or restored to the perfect state I have thus pointed out, has so much regularity in the general disposition of it, that the Work would appear to me as the wonderful production of the Roman art and power in Britain, in the most early ages of the world, had she not been famed, and soon obtained such a place in history, for the learning of her natives, as to make them capable of performing greater things, before the rise, even of the Grecian empire. Therefore I shall adventure to lay before you the substance of what I have collected, to explain the works of Stonehenge as a public building, whose venerable remains will always shine with the characters of art and immense labor, amongst those of the proudest structures that anciently graced the British empire; structures that drew the Gallic Druids into our island long before Cæsar advanced the Roman eagle to our shore; and structures that Egypt herself might glory in amidst her choicest examples of architecture.

How stupendous the public buildings of the ancient Britons were, and how much above the idea of mankind in general the performance of them was, seems every where to be handed down to the present age; common tradition, and even history itself, making the Devil, Conjurors, or Giants, to be the artificers who performed them.

The diameter of the body of this Structure is just one hundred and four feet; and the area about it, including the first bank of the earth, is of the same breadth; so that this part of the whole work is three hundred and twelve feet diameter, or thrice the diameter of the body of the Fabric; and this is environed with a ditch, and a second bank of earth.*

---

* Mr. Wood, in his finished plan of this Temple, makes the number of Stones amount to just one hundred and twenty-eight; and the area round the body of the work, an English acre and one quarter of land, capable of containing six thousand people, yielding a square yard for each person to stand on.

92

DR. SMITH.

Anno 1771.

STONEHENGE is a structure which strikes every beholder with wonder and amazement. From many and repeated visits I conceived it to be an Astronomical Temple; and from what I could recollect to have read of it, no Author had as yet investigated its uses. Without an instrument, or any assistance whatever, but White's Ephemeris, I began my survey. I suspected the stone called *The Friar's Heel*, to be the Index that would disclose the uses of this Structure; nor was I deceived. This stone stands in a right line with the centre of the Temple, pointing to the north-east. I first drew a circle round the vallum of the ditch, and divided it into 360 equal parts; and then a right line through the body of the Temple to the Friar's Heel; at the intersection of these lines, I reckoned the sun's greatest amplitude at the summer solstice, in this latitude, to be about 40 degrees, and fixed the eastern point accordingly. Pursuing this plan, I soon discovered the uses of all the detached stones, as well as those that formed the body of the Temple.

As the Spectator advances from the valley up the grand avenue to the Temple, the first Stone that offers to his view is called *The Friar's Heel*, and stands two hundred and ten feet from the body of the Structure, in the middle of the avenue, and in a right line with the grand entrance. The shape of this stone is pyramidal; sixteen feet four inches high, and twenty-four feet nine inches in circumference; it stands bowing towards the Temple, and has been much injured by the weather; there is not the least appearance of any tool upon it. When you view it from the centre of the Temple, it stands 5 degrees nearer to the east from the north-east.

One hundred feet beyond, in the same line with the last mentioned stone, lies another large Stone on the vallum of the ditch, twenty-one feet four inches long, seven feet broad, and three thick, sunk under the surface of the earth: this stone formerly stood erect, and was square at top. It is about eighty-five feet distant from the Temple.

The next Stone, by the vallum of the ditch, on the left hand, is near ninety feet from the Temple, and 80 degrees from the last mentioned stone; it was, when erect, ten feet six inches high, thirteen feet six inches in circumference, and of a pyramidal form. It leans very much towards the ditch, and stands just 40 degrees from the east.

Directly opposite to the last stone, stands another erect, four feet high, and eleven feet nine inches in circumference; ninety feet distant from the Temple, and 40 degrees from the west.

These are all the stones that are detached from the body of this venerable structure. The ditch is about one hundred and four feet from the Temple, and in most places about thirty feet wide; the earth for the most part is thrown inward which formed the vallum.

Directly north and south of the Temple, just within the vallum of the ditch, is the appearance of two circular holes, encompassed with the earth that was thrown out of them, but they are now almost effaced by time; they were, perhaps, first intended for a meridian line. All these Stones are of the rock kind, composed of a very strong grit, and so incrusted by time, that a tool will hardly touch them.

The outward circle of this Temple consisted of thirty upright stones, of a stupendous size, crowned with thirty architraves, or imposts.

The upright pillars with their imposts, are of the same kind of sand rock as those before-mentioned. Dr. Stukeley will have it to be a kind of bastard marble; but I must beg leave to dissent from him; and humbly hope to convince the Reader that it is a sand rock, composed of a very sharp grit, and so hardened by time, that at present it resists the force of any tool; they stand in a bed of chalk, which constantly drains off all moisture that falls on them. The upright pillars have each ot them two oval tenons, and the imposts two oval mortises to receive the tenons of the uprights. All the uprights are wrought on their beds.

These uprights are not all of an equal breadth; some measure seven feet wide, others less; the same as to the thickness, some being three feet and a half, others much less. The void space between the pillars is about three feet five inches; but those at the grand entrance stand at a greater distance. The imposts are about two feet six inches thick; and as they rather overhang the pillars, they are somewhat wider than the pillars.

The second circle, about nine feet and an half distant, and concentric with the first, consisted likewise of thirty stones, about seven feet high, but of no regular form, some being square at the basis, others oblong, and indeed of various shapes; and, as such, answered very well the purpose of the builder: they never were placed at equal distances from each other, nor covered with imposts. Some of these stones are of a dark mixed marble, of the granite kind, and extremely hard.

The intention of the Druids was, when they

erected this Temple, to give a phase of the moon when she was six days old, and an egg-like form to the earth; which could not have been formed without two centers, and which Dr. Stukeley seems to have had some notion of.

The next, and grandest part of this Structure, was originally an ellipsis, or oval. This grand ellipsis consisted of fourteen upright pillars, and seven architraves; they stood in pairs, detached at equal distances from each other; each pair of pillars was covered with an impost, or architrave : each pillar had one tenon; and each impost or architrave, two mortises to receive the tenons of the two pillars. Each pair of pillars stand about one foot or more from each other, the architrave spanning the breadth of the pillars, and are properly called trilithons by Dr. Stukeley.

The number of Stones, that composed this magnificent Temple, is as follows:

Uprights of the outward circle	30
Architraves over the same	30
The inward circle	30
The great oval	14
Architraves over the same	7
The inward oval	13
The altar	1
Three stones on the vallum	3
The large stone in the avenue	1
	129

The Stone in the middle of the grand avenue to the Temple, is the Key by which I propose to unlock this repository of Druidical secrets.

An horizon being drawn round the Temple, is divided into 360 equal parts, or degrees; the outward circle of the horizon is divided into 12 equal parts; each part marked with a Sign of the Zodiac. These signs stand 30 degrees from each other. Begin at the east with Aries, and reckon them on the right till you come to Pisces, the last sign. These are their names and characters:

Aries	♈	the Ram
Taurus	♉	the Bull
Gemini	♊	Twins
Cancer	♋	the Crab
Leo	♌	the Lion
Virgo	♍	the Virgin
Libra	♎	the Balance
Scorpio	♏	the Scorpion
Sagittarius	♐	the Centaur
Capricornus	♑	the horned Goat
Aquarius	♒	the Waterer
Pisces	♓	Fishes.

The Sun, in his annual revolution round his axis, passes through one of these Signs every month; in twelve months he passes through them all, and then the solar year is completed. At the summer solstice, when the days are longest, he enters the sign Cancer, and seems to rise in the same point of the horizon three days together. The Arch Druid standing against his stall, and looking down the right line of the Temple, his eye is bounded by Durrington Field, a charming horizon about two miles distant: he there sees the Sun rise from behind the hill. At this solstice the Sun rises 10 degrees in Taurus, and sets 20 degrees in Leo; his greatest amplitude (in this latitude) is 40 degrees at rising, and the same from the west at setting. At the winter solstice the Sun is in Capricorn, and rises 20 degrees in Aquarius, and sets 10 degrees in Scorpio; here is no stone to point out his setting. His greatest amplitude at rising, is 40 degrees south of the east, and the same amplitude at setting, south of the west.

F

97

The outward circle of the Temple consists of 30 pillars; these multiplied by the 12 Signs make 360, as many days as were reckoned in the ancient solar year; or at least I apprehend so. These pillars were crowned at top with a circular cornice of imposts. All circles were looked upon by the ancients as symbols of the Deity, of eternity, and of the revolution of time. The ancient Egyptians represented the year hieroglyphically, by a serpent with the tail in its mouth, which representation is continued down to us in our common Almanacs, with these mottos: " *In sese volvitur annus ; annus latet in angue.*" Whether or not the Druids allowed for the solstices in reckoning the days of the year, I cannot take upon me to say; they must certainly know the number of days and hours the year consisted of from this mathematical observatory. The division of the great circle into 360 degrees, is as ancient as their common parent Noah; if not many ages primæval to the deluge.

The inward circle is the lunar month; between it and the great ellipsis you see the phase of the moon when she is six days old; the Druids then began to reckon her days till she put on the same appearance again, which were twenty-nine days and twelve hours: here they had an opportunity of comparing the lunar months with the solar year.

At the upper end of this circle, there are Six Stones standing close together, by which are expressed the Harvest and Hunter's Moon; she, at these seasons, rises six nights together, with little variation, owing to the small angle she makes.

Next to this circle is the great Ellipsis, composed of seven pair of pillars, with an impost on each pair; I call them *The Seven Planets*, which at present give names to the seven days of the week; the reason why they are described by three stones, or trilithons, I apprehend to be this: The Druids conceived that each Planet had great influence over the seasons; they never gathered plants, &c. but under the aspects of one or other of them; a practice continued almost to our times by botanists of great repute. All nature is sensible of the genial warmth of the sun; the water of the seas would become stagnant, were it not for the moon's pressure on our atmosphere, which causes tides, and many other phœnomena unaccounted for; what influence the other planets may have over us, I must leave to the Reader. Whatever the Druids did was mysterious, and religiously kept from the knowledge of the vulgar; from thence I conclude, these trilithons expressed the three seasons of the year; the word autumn not being known in any of the Celtic languages, nor among the Jews; for in the holy Scriptures you have only seed time, harvest, and winter; or spring, summer, and winter. These Planets, with two stones of the inner circle, give that oviform or egg-like shape to the earth. This is the serpent's egg, or *ovum mundi* of the ancients, who were entirely ignorant from whence it proceeded. The Druids, in the creation of the world, conceived all nature to spring from this egg of the earth, which mystery they concealed from the world in other works besides this of Stonehenge.

To find out the elevation of the north pole, or latitude of the place: Draw a line through the Temple, and divide it into 90 equal parts, which is a quadrant of the great circle, and you will find the centre between the two focus's of the ellipsis to be 51 degrees and about 11 minutes; you will find also the latitude of this Temple to be the same in the Maps of Wiltshire. And what may seem more extraordinary, the Temple could not have been erected in this form in any other parallel of latitude. In order to prove it, draw two concentric circles about 11 degrees from each other; another circle must be

F 2

drawn, the lower part of which is to be formed with part of the second circle; so as to give a phase to the moon when she is six days old: the centre then, of this last circle, will be in 51 degrees and about 11 minutes north latitude.

If you attempt to draw the third circle in any other degree of latitude, it will either not touch the second circle, or become eccentric. Suppose, for instance, you draw a circle in 45 degrees of latitude (a place in Gaul, where the Druids held their national council, as Cæsar informs us in his Commentaries), it will be exactly concentric with the other two circles; if for the latitude of Petersburgh, it will be eccentric; so for Naples in Italy, and Alexandria in Egypt.

The stones called *The Thirteen Lunar Months*, or the Twelve Signs of the Zodiac, never stood equidistant from each other. The Druids undoubtedly had their reasons for it, which I suppose to be these: The Stone behind the Altar was assigned to the Arch Druid for his stall; Libra and Scorpio on each side of it, to those next in dignity; and so of the rest; the Druidesses probably attended on public occasions. Aries and Taurus, which stand at a much greater distance from the others, were intended for the Bards (the place at present assigned to the musicians in our choirs), where there was room sufficient for all their musical instruments, &c.

The last stone to be taken notice of is the *Altar*. On this Altar the Druids offered up the blood only of their sacrifices. Notwithstanding they have been charged by all authors with offering up human victims, I must beg leave to dissent from them, for the following reason: which is, that this Altar will not bear the fire. I tried a fragment of it in a crucible; it soon changed its blueish to an ash colour, and, in a stronger fire, was reduced to powder.

If what has been said is not sufficient to prove this a Tropical Temple, let us enquire into the derivation of its British name, *Choir Gaur.*

Choir, in all our Dictionaries is rendered *choire,* or quire of a church; the true sense of the word being lost in all the Celtic languages. Calashio, in his Hebrew Lexicon, translates the radical word *Chor* or *Cor, Concha Marina ;* which may, I presume, be called *Cancer,* the crab shell resembling more the quire of a church than any other, it being of an elliptic or oval form.

Gaur in the Irish, *Gauvr* in the Armoric, and *Gafr* in the Welsh, are words of the same sound, and signify *Caper* the he-goat; from whence *Capricorn,* the sign when the sun enters the winter solstice; and *Cancer,* when the sun enters the summer solstice.

I hope the Reader is now convinced of its being a Tropical Temple, erected by the ancient Druids for observing the motions of the heavenly bodies; and from whence probably the choirs of all churches derived their name.

These Stones are erected in the same rude state as when first taken from the quarry, there being no traces of tools on any of them, except on their beds, where they receive the imposts; and a little at the end of the imposts to favor the circular form of the Temple; and are far from being of an equal size, notwithstanding what some Authors have suggested.

KING.

FROM HIS MUNIMENTA ANTIQUA.

Anno 1799.

I CHANCED the first time I visited this Structure to approach it by moonlight; this, however, was a circumstance advantageous to the appearance; insomuch, that although my mind was previously filled with determined aversion, and a degree of horror, on reflecting upon the abominations of which this spot must have been the scene; and to which it even gave occasion in the latter periods of Druidism; yet it was impossible not to be struck, in the still of the evening, whilst the moon's pale light illumined all with reverential awe, at the solemn appearance produced by the different shades of this immense Group of astonishing masses of rock, artificially placed, impending over head with threatening aspect; bewildering the mind with the almost inextricable confusion of their relative situations with respect to each other; and, from their rudeness, as well as from their prodigious bulk, conveying at one glance, all the ideas of stupendous greatness, that could well be assembled together: whilst, at the same time, the vast expanse of landscape from this summit of an hill, added an idea of boundless magnificence, similar to that produced by a view of the wide extended ocean.

Surely, there can hardly be a more painful reflection, or one that more tends to cause an honest mind to shudder with indignation, than that by the perverseness and blindness of the human heart, such grand association of ideas should ever have been perverted to impious and idolatrous purposes, instead of being directed to the worship and honor of HIM, who created the whole expanse from hence surveyed, both above, and beneath; who made sun, moon, and stars; heavens, and heavens of heavens; worlds of inconceivable glory.

It is an happy circumstance, that we do not, at this distance of time, with precision, understand *what* the abominations here practised, in the latter most corrupted ages of Druidsm, were; though the first original designation, in conformity with Patriarchal usages, is manifest enough.

It is not to be lamented that we are so far ignorant; and it would be serving but an ill purpose to endeavour to bring them to light again; or to strive to catch ideas of them by the wild guidance of conjecture, as has sometimes been endeavoured.

I shall beg leave, therefore, here to draw the veil: and in these observations only to elucidate as much as appears most positively clear, from the most ancient records; and as is indeed, in a degree, free from any unnecessary concern with those gross abominations.

The Stones which are here found, are, in general (as far as such rude masses can be reduced to any scale) between six and seven feet broad; between three and four thick; and about fourteen in height; and, when they were all entire, plainly formed (as appears from the uniform proportions of what remain) a great circular inclosure of about ninety-seven feet in diameter, consisting of thirty upright rude stone pillars, and of thirty imposts, each of which was about ten feet long, or a little more, and about three feet thick. The intervals or inter-columniations between these stones was only about three, or sometimes near four feet: but amongst these, the interval which formed a sort of principal entrance to this august Structure was rather wider than the rest. The whole construction manifestly shewing, how even very small dimensions, provided there be but a sufficiently obvious scale for measuring the greatly different proportions of the several parts, may convey effectual ideas of magnificence, even detached from any consideration of the additional circumstance of grandeur that is conveyed by the vast bulk of each single stone.

There remain seventeen upright pillars of the outward circle standing; and seven now lying on the ground, either whole, or in pieces; there remain also six of the imposts in their places. But all the rest are carried off and lost.

They have all plainly in a degree been wrought with a tool; for, in order to join the upright pillars to the imposts more effectually, there is formed on the top of each pillar, a sort of tenon, of the form of half an egg, about ten inches and a half in diameter, which was made to fit into a corresponding mortise in the impost. And the rude pillars themselves, on examination, have been found to be placed at bottom in a kind of socket dug in the chalky soil, and having small flints carefully rammed in between the stone and the sides of the socket.

About nine feet nearer towards the centre; that is, nine feet from the inside of this exterior circle, appear the remains of a second and interior circle of smaller stones, which are of about one half of the dimensions of those of the outward circle; and (from the proportion of the distances of those that remain, as well as from their situation) they appear to have been originally twenty-nine in number. Only nine of these are now left standing in their proper places; and whether they ever had, or had not, imposts on them, is not at present to be determined. But it is remarkable, that as the stones of the outward circle are of a lightish colour, being by some observers deemed to be of the same kind as the *Grey-Wethers* on Salisbury Plain; these, of the inner circle, are of darker hue, almost inclining to black; which variety and contrast must have added much to the beauty of the original work.

After passing the remains of these two great outward circles, between which the circular walk seems to have been nearly three hundred feet in circumference, and to have afforded an awful view of the interior structure, we come to the most striking part of the whole, which is at the distance of about thirteen feet more inwards; consisting of a large portion of an oval, about fifty-two feet in its shortest diameter, and a few feet more in its longest; a part of whose circumference was formed originally by at least five (or as appeared to me, and as I much suspect, by seven) massy combinations of huge fragments of rock, in the form of exceeding high altars, placed one at the end, and the rest on each side of the longest diameter, fronting the principal entrance.

These Dr. Stukeley calls *trilithons*, because they were composed of three great stones each, and stand each quite apart, and not joined to, or appearing to have any annexation to each other, like the pillars and stones in the outward circle.

This vast rude remain of the highest trilithon is about twenty-two feet in length to its top, whereon still exists the great tenon that fastened it to the impost above. Its fellow supporter is thrown down, and lies just by, in two great pieces; whilst the impost itself is fallen quite across the long black stone which was placed a little before the foot of this high altar; and in this position it for some years re-

105

mained, so nicely balanced, as to form a sort of rocking stone.

All these great trilithons may be plainly observed to have been so constructed, that those on each side the oval were made respectively to increase in height the farther thay were from the entrance; whilst this (whose leaning pillar is left), which fronted the entrance, was highest of all.

In the front of this last, at the distance of about twelve feet, was placed on the very ground, and partly sunk into it, a great black stone, about sixteen feet in length, and four feet wide, and about twenty inches thick; which seems to have marks of burning upon it still remaining; and is of a quite different, and harder kind of stone than the rest, as being designed to resist the effects of fire.

The leaning pillar of the great and' highest trilithon, and the two trilithons on each side, remained entire when I visited the spot; and whilst the vastness of their bulk is so obvious, it cannot but appear most remarkable, what a very small interval there is between the two great supporters of each trilithon: it is not more than twenty-one, or twenty-two inches, though the width of each stone supporter is at least about seven feet, or seven and a half. This narrow interval, therefore, seems plainly to indicate, that the void space between the two stones could neither have been designed for a seat, as some have supposed; or for any entrance; or for passing through for any superstitious purposes, as others have imagined: but that plainly, each structure of these five was intended, indeed, solely for an high raised basis; an altar of oblation; a sort of table of offerings; according to what we read of ancient ceremonies concerning offerings; and are informed is still in use amongst barbarous and Gentile nations.

WANSEY.

Anno 1796.

By whom this venerable ancient Structure was erected, or on what occasion, is difficult in this remote age of the world to determine. It is mentioned by British writers more than a thousand years ago; yet it is remarkable that neither Suetonius, nor Dio, who wrote so much concerning the British Druids; Tacitus, nor Ptolemy, who wrote largely of British affairs; nor any Roman writer whatever; nor Cæsar; make any mention of it; yet it is clear that it existed before their time, because a Roman road, still visible, cuts off a large corner of one of the barrows. But the Romans, it should seem, held in contempt all the temples and edifices of the Barbarians, as they affected to call all other nations; and even the beautiful edifices of Athens and Corinth were destroyed by them without any compunction. A Roman camp, capable of holding ten thousand men, is still visible within five miles of Stonehenge (Yarnbury Castle), believed by Camden to be a station of Vespasian's, who is said by Suetonius to have fought thirty battles, conquered two powerful nations in this quarter, and reduced the Isle of Wight to the power of the Romans; for which the Senate decreed the Emperor Claudius the honor of a triumph, and instituted civic games. The various Writers since have differed so much about its origin, that while some have ascribed it to the Druids, the Britons, the Romans, the Saxons, and the Danes, others have carried its origin farther back than the creation of Adam. Mr. Waltire, who wrote, and delivered lectures, on Stonehenge, endeavours to demonstrate that it has been immerged in the sea twelve miles deep; and that it was erected, judging by the precession of the equinox, at least seventeen thousand years ago.

The most ancient writer who makes any mention of Stonehenge, is Ninnius (Gibson says it is mentioned in some manuscripts of Ninnius), a disciple of Elvodugus, who flourished about the year 617; an author of good antiquity, says Camden. This was at least two hundred years before the Danes had acquired any considerable part of the island, consequently they could not be the authors of it; however, as he does not attempt to explain its origin, it is not probable it was erected to perpetuate the treachery of Hengist the Saxon, in assassinating the British nobles at a feast given near that spot by Vortigern, about the year 450.

Amidst the variety of these conjectures, it would be vanity indeed, in any Writer of the present day, to pretend to satisfy the enquiring mind on this subject. The best thing he can do, is to trace out the opinions of the various Writers from the most ancient times to the present, and after that to state such facts and discoveries upon opening the barrows, and digging near Stonehenge, as have from attentive reading and observation come to his knowledge.

Stonehenge is a modern name compared with its original one, which was *Choir Gaur*. This some of the Monkish Writers have turned into Latin, and rendered *Chorea Gigantum*, not being able to adopt a better name. This ancient British name is well known and understood by the Welshmen of the present day, but does not properly explain its origin.

A circular ditch round Stonehenge is still visible, and its distance is just one hundred and four feet from the stones; one hundred and fifty feet from the ditch to the middle of the Temple; and three hundred from ditch to ditch across the middle of the Temple.

The stones of the outward ring to the northward are fourteen feet in height, while those on the south side are only thirteen, because the ground is higher on that side; and this is nicely and accurately contrived by the ancient builders of it to keep the cross stone over them to the same elevation, so as to describe an elevated circle parallel to the horizon to the eye of an Observer standing near the Altarstone. *(this is a curious fact.)* The highest of the stones now standing is in the inner circle, and measures twenty-two feet, and that leans on a little pillar which has a groove in it : of these little pillars there were, it is believed, thirty, as well as thirty uprights in the outer circle. The stone called *The Friar's Heel* stands two hundred and ten feet distant from the Temple, and measures in height sixteen feet four inches, in circumference twentyfour feet nine inches.

If you stand by the Altar-stone,* and look towards the Friar's Heel, you will see that the top of that stone coincides with Durrington Hill; and on the top of that stone the Sun is supposed to make its first appearance on the longest day of the year; but from a certain motion of the earth, called the precession of the equinox, it is considerably departed from it, equal to a fourth part of a revolution, which, according to Ptolemy's calculation, requires seventy thousand years to perform.

A Tin Tablet, with an illegible inscription on it, was dug up at Stonehenge about the year 1540;

---

* Dr. Smith observes, that the Altar-stone will not bear fire. I have tried it in the strongest heat, and find it will.

G

it was shewn to Sir Thomas Elliot, and to Lilly, but they could make nothing out of it.

Several Brass Celts have been found in opening different barrows; and Bones, sometimes in rude-shaped urns of clay, at other times without them, both burnt and unburnt, of men, horses, oxen, and dogs; also Beads, Trinkets, and bits of Coral and Amber. Of the Bodies found, it was observed the head was always placed northward.

In the year 1635 a large quantity of pewter was found in plowing near Normanton ditch; which sold as old pewter for several pounds.

Though Brass and Tin, Amber and Beads, have been frequently found, it is not known that any *Iron* article was ever dug up at Stonehenge; a strong presumption that it must have been erected before the use of iron was known in Britain.

Stonehenge stands in the best situation possible for observing the heavenly bodies, as there is an horizon nearly three miles distant on all sides; and on either distant hill trees might have been so planted as to have measured any number of degrees of a circle, so as to calculate the right ascension, or declination of a star or planet. But till we know the methods by which the ancient Druids calculated eclipses long before they happened, so as to have made their astronomical observations with so much accuracy as Cæsar mentions, we cannot explain the theoretical uses of Stonehenge. It is therefore no proof that Stonehenge was not intended for calculating the motions of the heavenly bodies, because no present method of making observations is to be applied to the Druids. Their geometrical skill, notwithstanding, cannot be doubted.

Robertson, in the Appendix to his *History of India,*

says, " The method of predicting eclipses followed by the Bramins, is of a kind altogether different from any found amongst the nations of Europe. In Chaldea also, as well as Greece, in early ages, the method of calculating eclipses was founded on the observation of a certain period, or cycle, after which the sun and the moon agree with their former calculations."

Monsieur Bailly, the celebrated astronomer, and unfortunate Mayor of Paris, maintained, " That none of all the astronomical systems of Greece, of Persia, or of Tartary, can be made to agree with the Indian tables, which, however, though calculated back to remote ages, are found quite as accurate as ours. The place of the sun for the astronomical epoch at the beginning of the Calyougham in the year 3102 before Christ, as stated in the tables of Tirvalore, is only forty-seven minutes greater than in the tables of M. de la Caille, when corrected by the calculations of M. de la Grange."

Was a learned Brahmin to contemplate on the Ruins of Stonehenge, he might, possibly, comprehend more of its design than we do, and trace some vestiges of an art wholly unknown to us.

FALL OF THREE STONES,

In a Letter from Dr. MATON, to A. B. LAMBERT, Esq.
Dated May 30, 1797.

HAVING lately had more leisure to make Remarks on the Alteration produced in the aspect of Stonehenge, by the Fall of some of the Stones in January last, than when I first visited the spot for this purpose; I am anxious to lay before the Antiquarian Society a more full and correct account of it than that which you did me the honor to transmit to them before.

On the Third of the month already mentioned, some people employed at plough, full half a mile distant from Stonehenge, suddenly felt a considerable concussion, or jarring, of the ground, occasioned, as they afterwards perceived, by the Fall of Two of the largest Stones and their Impost. That the concussion should have been so sensible will not appear incredible, when I state the weight of these stones; but it may be proper to mention, first, what part of the Structure they composed, and what were their respective dimensions.

Of those five sets, or *compages*, of stones (each consisting of two uprights and an impost), which Dr. Stukeley expressively termed *trilithons*, three had hitherto remained in their original position, and entire, two being on the left hand side as you advance from the entrance towards the Altar-stone, and one on the right. The last mentioned *trilithon*[*] is now levelled with the ground. It fell outwards, nearly in a western direction, the impost in its fall striking against one of the stones of the outer circle, which, however, has not been thereby driven very

---

[*] This *trilithon* might, with great propriety, be called the western, as n one of the others stood more nearly west of the centre of the structure.

considerably out of its perpendicularity. The lower ends of the two uprights, or supporters, being now exposed to view, we are enabled to ascertain the form into which they were hewn. They are not right-angled, but bevilled off in such a manner that the stone which stood nearest to the upper part of the *adytum* is twenty-two feet in length on one side, and not quite twenty on the other; the difference between the corresponding sides of the fellow-supporter is still greater, one being as much as twenty-three, and the other scarcely nineteen feet, in length. The breadth of each is (at a medium) seven feet nine inches, and the thickness three feet. The impost, which is a perfect parallelopipedon, measures sixteen feet in length, four feet six inches in breadth, and two feet six inches in thickness.

Now, a cubic inch of the substance * of which the above stones are composed, weighing, according to my experiments, one ounce six pennyweights, the ponderosity of the entire *trilithon* will be found to be nearly seventy tons. The impost alone is considerably more than eleven ton in weight. This stone, which was projected about two feet beyond the supporters, made an impression in the ground to the depth of seven inches, or more; it was arrested in its tendency to roll by the stone it struck whilst falling. The supporters, of course, have not sunk so deep; indeed, one of them fell on a stone belonging to the second circle, which I at first supposed to have been thrown down by it, but which, from recurring to the plans of the prior state of the Structure, I find have long been prostrate.

Though I could not contemplate without emotions of peculiar awe and regret, such an assault of

---

* This is a filiceous grit, of rather a loose texture, and of a dull whitish colour, with veins of brown, which seem to be occasioned by the oxydation of the iron contained in it. All the stones of the great oval, and most of those of the outer circle, consist of this species of rock.

G 3

time and the elements on this venerable Structure, I must own these emotions were in some measure counterbalanced by the satisfaction of being now enabled to discover the original depth of these stupendous Stones in the ground. It appears that the longer of the supporters was not more than three feet six inches deep (measuring down the middle), nor the other but little more than three feet. In the cavities left in the ground, there are a few fragments of stone of the same nature as that forming the substance of the trilithon, and some masses of chalk. These materials seem to have been placed here with a view to secure the perpendicular position of the supporters.

The immediate cause of this memorable change in the state of Stonehenge, must have been the sudden and rapid thaw that began the day before the stones fell, succeeding a very deep snow. In all probability the trilithon was *originally* perfectly upright, but it had acquired some degree of inclination long before the time of its fall. This inclination was remarked by Dr. Stukeley, though it was not so considerable, I think, as is represented in his north view of Stonehenge. One of the supporters had lost much of its original bulk, in consequence of corrosion by the weather, near its foundation; this circumstance also rendered it less secure. As both had so inconsiderable a depth in the ground, a sudden, though slight, diminution of the pressure of the latter against the inclining side must appear to have been fully sufficient, on account of the shock which the impost would suffer, to occasion the downfal of the whole.

We do not find the precise time of any alteration prior to this upon record; it is therefore probable that none may have happened for several centuries, and the late accident being the only circumstance ascertained with exactness, may be considered as a remarkable æra in the History of this noble Monument of ancient art.

SIR R. C. HOARE.

FROM HIS ANCIENT HISTORY OF S. WILTSHIRE.

Anno 1812.

THIS remarkable Monument is situated on the open down, near the extremity of a triangle formed by two roads; the one leading on the south from Amesbury to Wily, the other on the north from the same place, through Shrewton and Heytesbury, to Warminster.

A building of such obscure origin, and of so singular a construction, has naturally attracted the attention of the learned, and numerous have been the publications respecting it; conjectures have been equally various, and each author has formed his own.

It is a melancholy consideration, that at a period when the sciences are progressively advancing, and when newly discovered manuscripts are continually drawn forth from their cloistered retreats, to throw a light on the ancient records of our country; it is mortifying, I say, that the history of so celebrated a monument as Stonehenge, should still remain veiled in obscurity. The Monks may boldly assert that Merlin, and only Merlin, was the founder of our Temple; and we cannot contradict, though we may disbelieve. The revolution of ages frequently elucidates history, and brings many important facts to light; but here all is darkness and uncertainty: we may admire; we may conjecture; but we are doomed to remain in ignorance and obscurity.

The construction and plan of Stonehenge, are of so novel and singular a nature, that no verbal description, though drawn up by the ablest writer;

can possibly convey to the Reader a competent idea of it.

I cannot allow of more than one entrance into the area of the Work. This faces the north-east, and is decidedly marked by a bank and ditch, called the Avenue, which leads directly into it. On our approach to it on this side, the first object that arrests our attention, is a large rude stone in a leaning position, which by some has been called *The Friar's Heel*. Its height is about sixteen feet, and its original purport is totally unknown, though conjecture has not been idle in ascribing various uses to it.

Let us now approach this mysterious Building, and enter within its hallowed precincts. At first sight all is amazement and confusion; the eye is surprised, the mind bewildered. The stones begin now, and not before, to assume their proper grandeur; and the interior of the Temple, hitherto blinded by an uniform exterior, displays a most singular variety and gigantic magnificence.

This Temple consists of two circles and two ovals; the two latter constituting the Cell, or Sanctum. The outward circle, about three hundred feet in circumference, is composed of huge upright stones, bearing others over them, which form a kind of architrave. Though they evidently shew the mark of tools, they are still irregular in their forms and sizes. The height of the stones on each side of the entrance, is a little more than thirteen feet; and the breadth of one, seven feet; and of the other, six feet four inches; the impost over them is about two feet eight inches deep. The space between the stones in this outward circle varies; that between the entrance stones is five feet, and rather wider than in the rest. This circle consisted originally of thirty stones, of which seventeen still remain standing. At the distance of eight feet three inches from the inside of this outward circle, we find another composed of smaller stones, rude and irregular in their shapes.

We come now to the grandest part of our Temple, the Cell, or Sanctum; in forming which the general plan has been varied; for this inner Temple represents two-thirds of a large oval, and a concomitant small oval, as in the outward Temple we find a large and a small circle. The large oval is formed by five pair of trilithons, or two large upright stones, with a third laid over them as an impost. The placing of the imposts is also varied, for they are not continued all round, as in the outward circle, but are divided into pairs, thereby giving a great lightness to the work, and breaking its uniformity; neither are they like those of the outward circle, parallel at top; but they rise gradually in height from east to west.

Such indeed is the general fascination imposed on all those who view Stonehenge, that no one can quit its precincts without feeling strong sensations of surprise and admiration. The ignorant Rustic will with a vacant stare attribute it to the Giants, or the mighty Archfiend; and the Antiquary, equally uninformed as to its origin, will regret that its history is veiled in perpetual obscurity. The Artist, on viewing these enormous masses, will wonder that art could thus rival nature in magnificence and picturesque effect. Even the most indifferent Passenger over the plain must be attracted by the solitary and magnificent appearance of these Ruins; and all with one accord will exclaim, How grand! How wonderful! How incomprehensible!

———————

We lament that our limits will not permit us to make very copious extracts from this valuable work, or to accompany the learned Author in all his laborious and persevering researches within the bowels of the numerous Barrows which he caused to be opened for discovery. Nothing, however, appeared which could throw the most glimmering light on this mysterious Fabric; and which, therefore, must unfortunately remain without the least brightning prospect, clouded in obscurity. But truth is at length obtained, by the opening so many Barrows, as to the purposes for which they were formed. Their dimensions and depths were various, some being very shallow, whilst others were nearly fifteen feet deep. They generally produced one or more human skeletons; but those of early æra were frequently discovered to have been interred within a cist, with the legs drawn up towards the head. Bones, loose on the floors of the Barrows, burnt and unburnt, and sometimes in cists; numerous beads of amber, glass, stone, and horn; drinking cups of various sizes, were very common, and appeared to have been made with very poor clay, intermixed with bits of chalk, with the exception of two or three, which were richly ornamented; rude urns, containing various kinds of burned bones; sepulchral urns, of which some were in a very perfect state; pottery; ivory pins and tweezers; brass daggers, spear heads, and pins; a remarkable cist, made of the trunk of an elm tree, the wood and bark appearing fresh and perfect; spear heads and arrows of flint; large pieces of stags' horns; curious whetstones; and two knives, which were both found in the same barrow. *

---

* On erecting Shrewton wind mill, distant about four miles south west of Stonehenge, the interment (though not a barrow) of a skeleton was discovered, together with several brass articles, a drinking cup, and the blade of an iron knife This interment appears of a later æra, when the custom of gathering up the legs had ceased, and when the use of iron was more generally adopted, for in the early tumuli none of that metal has ever been found. The same observations may be applied to the barrow at Stonehenge which contained the two knives.

THE DRUIDS.

WE shall conclude our Description of that re-markable piece of antiquity, Stonehenge, with an Account of the DRUIDS, by whom it is supposed to have been erected.

The Druids were a body of men, who, though generally considered as Priests, acted in a civil as well as ecclesiastical capacity. The reason of their becoming possessed of secular as well as clerical authority, was owing to a notion being prevalent among the people, that none ought to submit to punishment for any crime whatever but by divine authority; which authority was delegated to, and lodged in the priesthood only. Hence the Druids had an uncontrouled power over the mind and persons of the laity. Exempted from taxes, excused from military services, arbitrators in civil concerns, judges in criminal matters, and public oracles of the community, it must be imagined that their sentences were without appeal; indeed few dared dispute their infallibility. But if by chance an individual had so much temerity, he was punished by an excommunication so dreadful, as to be deemed more terrible than the most cruel death: from that moment he was considered as a person abandoned by God and man; universally hated and condemned, no one would associate with him; but he was suffered to drag through a miserable existence till penury or sorrow snatched him from a world in which he could neither obtain pity or relief.

The Druids were under no apprehension that their influence could ever decline: being solely in-

119

trusted with the education of youth, they from infancy secured the respect of the people, and implanted that awe in their juvenile breasts which increased with their years, and at length ripened into the most permanent and profound veneration.

The Druids were of three classes, *viz.* Druids properly so called, Bards, and Eubates or Vates.

The first class presided over and regulated all public affairs, both in spirituals and temporals; their decisions were final over life and effects, and a principal part of their business was to direct and adjust all public sacrifices, and religious ceremonies. They were under the direction of a Principal elected by themselves, and styled Archdruid, whose authority extended so as to call to account, and depose the secular Prince, whenever he thought proper.

The second class, or Bards, were the national Preceptors, having the care of educating the children of both sexes, and all ranks. It was likewise their business to compose verses in commemoration of their heroes and other eminent people, and to furnish songs upon all public occasions, which they sung to the sound of harps.

The third class, Eubates, were skilled in physic, natural philosophy, astronomy, magic, divination, augury, &c.

Hence it appears that the Druids possessed, not only all the power and learning, but the principal archives, and places of trust in the nation; for they were the only priests, magistrates, preceptors, poets, musicians, physicians, philosophers, orators, astronomers, magicians, &c. in the kingdom. It is not therefore surprising that the principal people should be ambitious to get their children and relations admitted into their classes; and that the vulgar should regard them with as much veneration as they did their deities, whose immediate agents they imagined they were.

If any disturbance ever happened among the Druids, it was upon the death of the Primate, when such earnest endeavours were made to get appointed to that honorable and powerful office, that the freedom of election was frequently disturbed by appeals to the sword; upon all other occasions they acted with great justice, moderation, disinterestedness, and temperance, which at once secured that respect the people naturally entertained for them.

Their adoration and religious ceremonies were performed in groves consecrated to their deities. These groves were composed of, surrounded by, and fenced in with lofty oak trees; as they held sacred that towering monarch of the British plains. Though the reason of such prepossession in favor of this tree, in particular, is now unknown, yet it is remarkable, that the ancient rustic natives of this island should adore that tree as a sacred production of the earth, which the more refined modern inhabitants ought to revere as their principal bulwark on the main.

" The Druids," says Pliny, " had such an esteem for the oak, that they would not suffer any religious ceremony to be performed without being embellished with garlands made of its leaves. These philosophers believe that it is the chosen tree of God, and that whatever grows upon it cometh from Heaven." The misletoe, which nature had taught to grow on and embrace the sturdy oak, came in for a share of their veneration; they deemed it the peculiar gift of Providence, and held its virtues universal in medicine. It was yearly sought for, particularly on the first day of the first new moon in the year, which was one of their most solemn festivals, when a proper

H

branch of that arboreous plant being selected, the Arch-Druid mounted the tree to which it clung, cut it off with a golden knife, and carefully wrapped it up in his garments, amidst the joyous acclamations of the enraptured multitude, who deemed it the happy omen of a prosperous year. The Arch-Druid, whose residence was at Mona, now the Isle of Anglesea, in North Wales, from the nature and extent of his authority, may be considered as the Metropolitan, or the Pontiff, of the Britons.

The religious tenets which the Druids taught the people teemed with the grossest superstitions, and enjoined human sacrifices as oblations to their deities. The first part they had in common with the Celts and Gauls, and the latter they learned from the Phœnicians. Their deities were, Jupiter, Apollo, Mars, Mercury, Andates their goddess of victory, and others of a subordinate class to them. After the Roman invasion they added Minerva, Diana, and Hercules. Their worship consisted in human and other sacrifices, expiatory oblations, invocations, and thanksgivings. They had, in common with other idolatrous people, both ancient and modern, the custom of making their idols hideously ugly, which evinces that idolatry in general was, and still is, formed more on fear than love; as the figures which image-worshippers are universally pleased to give to their deities, seem rather calculated to excite horror, or ridicule, than to inspire reverence and respect. Unacquainted with the awful and amiable attributes of the true Deity, ignorant and barbarous nations, in all ages, have formed their religious opinions more on apprehension than admiration, and being incapable of conceiving the nature of true benevolence, have sought a remedy for their fears in the partial deprecation of wrath.

All Druidical ceremonies, and literary precepts, were performed and delivered extempore, as they never suffered either their maxims or their sciences to be committed to writing. This restriction was founded on two motives; the one that the vulgar should not become acquainted with their mysterious learning by means of any manuscripts which might accidentally fall into their hands; and the other, that the extensive faculties of their pupils might be invigorated by continual exercise.

Though the idolatry of the Druids was abominable, and their human sacrifices execrable, yet their moral philosophy hath been the admiration of after ages; and many of their maxims which stand recorded have met with eulogiums of the most celebrated and polished writers.

South-East View of Stonehenge.

3.
Stonehenge, Temple of the Druids

John Aubrey, in these edited extracts
from his *Monumenta Britannica*
(eventually published in 1980-82,
transcribed by Rodney Legg and John
Fowles), associated Stonehenge with
the Druid myth and the two have
remained entwined for three
centuries

THERE HAVE been several books writ by learned men
concerning Stonehenge, much differing from one another,
some affirming one thing, some another. Now I come in
the rear of all by comparative arguments, to give a clear
evidence that these monuments were pagan temples:
which was not made-out before, and here also (with
humble subscription to better judgment) offered a probability that they were Temples of the Druids.

When a traveller rides along by the ruins of a
monastery, he knows by the manner of the building, that is
chapel, cloisters &c, that it was a convent, but of what
order (that is Benedictine, Dominican &c) it was, he
cannot tell by the bare view. So it is clear, that all the
monuments which I have here recounted, were temples.
Now my presumption is, that the Druids being the most
eminent priests (or order of priests) among the Britons, 'tis
odd , but that these ancient monuments were temples of
the priests of the most eminent order, viz. Druids, and, it is
strongly to be presumed that Avebury, Stonehenge &c are
as ancient as those times.

This inquiry I must confess is a groping in the dark:
but although I have not brought it into a clear light; yet I
can affirm, that I have brought it from an utter darkness to
a thin mist: and have gone farther in this essay than anyone
before me.

These antiquities are so exceeding old, that no
books do reach them; so that there is no way to retrieve
them but by comparative antiquity, which I have writ
upon the spot, from the monuments themselves ....

In the year 1655, was published by Mr John Webb

a book entitled *Stonehenge Restored* (but writ by Mr Inigo Jones) which I read with great delight; there is a great deal of learning in it: but having compared his scheme with the monument itself, I found he had not dealt fairly: but had made a Lesbian's rule [*mason's lead measure, for bending round mouldings*] which is conformed to the stone: that is, he framed the monument to his own hypothesis, which is much differing from the thing itself. This gave me an edge to make more researches.

Had this been a work of the Romans, certainly they would have made this cell of some harmonical figure; the ruins of it do clearly enough show (without further demonstration) that it could neither be a hexagon, or heptagon: nor can all the angles be forced to touch a circle. He supposes an altar stone; here are stones fallen down, this supposed altar being one of them. Perhaps they used no altar; for I find the middle of these monuments void.

Memorandum, a heptagon is a difficult figure to be made: and is not beautiful as a hexagon, which is most easily made: by applying the radius to the periphery. Why might not then, the seven-sided figure in the foregoing scheme be made in relation to the seven planets, and seven days of the week? I cannot determine: I can only suggest.

Dr Walter Charleton, physician to King Charles II, wrote a book entitled *Stonehenge Restored to the Danes*, wherein he hath showed a great deal of learning in a very good style: but as to his hypothesis, that it was a work of the Danes, it is a gross mistake: for Matthew Paris expressly affirms, that Stonehenge was the place where the Saxons' treachery massacred the Britons, which was ... hundred years before the conquest by the Danes. I think Simeon of Durham [*12th century chronicler*] and Henry of Huntingdon [*also of that period, author of Historia Anglorum*] say the same, vide [*which see*].

Such vast perennial memorials, seem rather to be a work of a people settled in their country, than of such roving pirates, who for their own security must be continually upon their guard, and consequently have but small leisure or reason for erecting such lasting monuments. And that we find also these monuments in the mountains of Caernarvonshire, and diverse other places, where no history does inform us, nor conjecture suggest, that ever the Danes have been. To which may be added, that if we compare strictly the Danish and Swedish monuments, we shall find a considerable difference in the order and structure of them. I find none of them compare to that magnificent tho' barbarous monument, on Salisbury Plain.

The Romans had no dominion in Ireland, or in Scotland (at least not far): therefore these temples are not to be supposed to be built by them: nor had the Danes dominion in Wales: and therefore we cannot presume the temples to have been works of them. But all these monuments are of the same fashion, and antique rudeness; wherefore I conclude, that they were works erected by the Britons: and were temples of the Druids.

Upon what ground the writers call it Stonehenge, I cannot tell: I have not seen the old deeds of this estate: but by the neighbourhood it is called Stone-edge, i.e. stones set edgewise.

The tradition amongst the common people is that these stones were brought from Ireland by the conjuration of Merlin (brother of Uther Pendragon) whereas indeed they are of the very same kind of stones, with the Grey wethers [*sarsen stones*] about fourteen miles off: that tract of ground towards Marlborough (from hence) being scattered over with them (as by a volcano) for about twenty miles in compass. They are so hard that no tool can touch, and take a good polish: some are of a dirty red, some dusky white, some perfect white, and I have seen some few blue, of the colour of deep blue marble, but generally they are whitish: they lie above the surface of the earth: they say the porphyry [*felspathic crystalline rock*] is not drawn out of quarries, but lies above ground after this manner.

But the stones of this monument (as likewise the Grey wethers) time and weather have made of a grey colour, as it doth also the flints that have been broken by the plough. Several of the high stones of Stonehenge are honeycombed so deep, that the stares [*starlings*] make their nests in the holes: whether those holes are natural or artificial I cannot say. The inhabitants about the Amesburys have defaced this piece of antiquity since my remembrance: one large stone was carried away to make a bridge.

It is generally averred hereabout that pieces (or powder) of these stones put into their wells, do drive away the toads, with which their wells are much infested, and this of course they use still. It is also averred, that no magpie, toad, or snake was ever seen here: but this is easy to be believed: for birds of weak flight will not go beyond their power of reaching some covert for fear of their enemies, hawks and ravens: whereas no covert is near a mile and a half of this place. As for the toads, they will not go beyond a certain distance from water by reason of spawning; and snakes and adders do love covert [cover].

George Duke of Buckingham, when King James the first was at Wilton [1620] did cause the middle of Stonehenge to be digged; and there remains a kind of pit or cavity still; it is about the bigness of two saw-pits, and this under-digging was the cause of the falling down or recumbency of the great stone there, twenty one foot long. He also caused then a barrow (or more than one) to be digged, where something was found, but what it was Mrs Mary Trotman (the wife of Mr Anthony Trotman, who lived then at the farm of West Amesbury, to which this monument belongs) to whom I am obliged for her very good information of this place, hath forgot. She told me, that the Duke of Buckingham would have given to Mr Newdick (then owner of this place) any rate for it, but he would not accept it.

The above account of Stonehenge is from John Aubrey's *Monumenta Britannica*, written between 1663 and 1693. Our compilation of extracts, given with modernised spellings, is from the first edition of this work, *Monumenta Britannica Volume One*, published by Dorset Publishing Company in 1980. It may help scholars if we identify the locations of these extracts within that work. Paragraphs one to three above are from pages 24 and 25.

Paragraph four is from page 26. Paragraphs five and six are from page 20. Paragraph seven from page 82. Paragraph eight is from page 85. Paragraph nine is from page 125. Paragraph ten is from page 129. Paragraph eleven is from pages 86 and 87. Paragraph twelve is from page 91. Paragraphs thirteen and fourteen are from pages 92 and 93. Paragraph fifteen is from pages 94 and 95.

4.
The Natural History of Stonehenge

Benjamin Martin's account of
Stonehenge was published in Volume
III of *The General Magazine of Arts and
Sciences*, for 1756. He concludes: "That
it is possible they might be made by
art, no man can dispute, who
considers, that the substance of
common stones, reduced to powder
and mixed with proper ingredients will
compose a substance that shall appear
like stone, and at the same time be
harder and heavier"

The Front View of STONEHENGE

A Geometrical Ground plot of Stonehenge.

The NATURAL HISTORY

Of STONEHENGE.

THIS celebrated Piece of Antiquity has employed the Pens of many of the Curious and Learned: but almost all who have written upon it, have varied in their Sentiments of its Antiquity, and the Use for which it was designed. We shall not here mention the Opinions of all the different Authors who have written on this Subject: It is sufficient here to observe, that the celebrated *Inigo Jones* endeavoured to prove that it is the Remains of a Temple, of the *Tuscan* Order, built by the *Romans* to the God *Cœlum* or *Terminus*; but that the ingenious Dr. *Stukeley*, has in a Manner proved, from various Considerations, that it was a Temple built by the antient *Britons*.*

This wonderful Edifice received its present Name from the *Saxons*, *Rode Hengenne*, or *Hanging Rocks*; and in *Yorkshire*, hanging Rocks are still called *Henges*.

Scarcely any thing can be more delightful than the Situation of this antient Monument. " Nothing can be sweeter than " the Air which moves over this hard, dry and chalky Soil. " Every Step you take upon the smooth Carpet, the Nose is sa- " luted with the fragrant Smell of *Serpillum* and *Apium*, which " with the short Grass, continually cropt by the Flocks of " Sheep, composes the softest and most verdant Turf, which " rises, as with a Spring, under one's Feet." It has the River *Avon* to the East, and a Brook that runs into the *Willy* on the West, which Streams encompass it half round, at the Distance of two Miles, forming, as it were, a circular Area of four or five Miles Diameter, composed of gentle Acclivities and Declivities,

* This learned Antiquary, among other Observations, takes Notice, that whoever erects any eminent Building, most certainly forms it upon the common Measure in Use, among the People of that Place, and therefore if the Proportions of *Stonehenge* fall into Fractions when measured by the *English*, *French*, *Roman*, or *Grecian* Foot, we may assuredly conclude, that the Architects were neither- *English*, *French*, *Romans* or *Greeks*: but that as *Stonehenge*, and all the other Works of this Nature in our Island, are erected by that most antient Measure called a Cubit, which was used by the *Hebrews*, *Egyptians* and *Phœnicians*, it must be built by the antient *Druids*, who probably came into *Britain* under the Conduct of the *Egyptian*, *Tyrian*, or *Phœnician Hercules* (who was the same Person) about *Abraham*'s Time, or soon after.

ties, open and airy; yet agreeably diverſified with the View of a Number of Barrows ſcattered over the higheſt Grounds.

Stonehenge ſtands near the Summit of a Hill, which riſes with a very gentle Aſcent. At the Diſtance of half a Mile it has a ſtately and auguſt Appearance; and as we advance nearer, eſpecially up the Avenue on the North-Eaſt Side, where the Remains of this wonderful Structure is moſt perfect, the Greatneſs of its Contour fills the Eye in an aſtoniſhing Manner. The Greatneſs of the Circuit of the whole Work; the Height of the Parts of which it is compoſed; and the Greatneſs too of the Lights and Shades, as well as their Variety, ariſing from its circular Form, gives it all poſſible Advantage. No one thinks any Part of it too great or too little, too high or too low. And we, that can only view it in its Ruins, the leſs regret thoſe Ruins, that, if poſſible, add to its ſolemn Majeſty.

Stonehenge is encompaſſed with a circular Ditch, the *Vallum* of which is inwards, and makes a circular Terras around the Area or Court. After this Ditch is paſſed, we proceed 108 Feet and ſomething more to the Work itſelf, which is 108 Feet in Diameter. " When you enter the Building, whether on Foot " or on Horſeback, and caſt your Eyes on the yawning Ruins, you " are ſtruck with an extatic Reverie, which none can deſcribe, " and they only can be ſenſible of that feel it. When we ad- " vance further, the dark Part of the ponderous Impoſts over " our Heads, the Chaſm of Sky between the Jambs of the Cell, " the odd Conſtruction of the whole, and the Greatneſs of " every Part ſurpriſes. If you look upon the perfect Part, you " fancy intire Quarries mounted up into the Air: if upon the " rude Havock below, you ſee, as it were, the Bowels of a " Mountain turned inſide outwards."

* The Stones of which this Temple is compoſed, were (ſays Dr. *Stukeley*) without Doubt brought from the *Grey Weathers* upon *Marlborough* Downs, near *Aubury*, where there is another wonderful Work of the ſame Kind. All the greater Stones are of this Sort, except the Altar, which is ſtill harder, as deſigned to reſiſt Fire. The Pyramids are likewiſe of a different Sort, and much harder than the reſt. If we conſider the prodigious Size of theſe Stones, and the Diſtance of the *Grey Weathers*, which is 16 Miles from

O this

* Dr. *Stukeley*'s *Stonehenge* reſtored to the *Britiſh* Druids.

this Place, the Difficulty of bringing them hither muſt be inconceivably great. The Stone at the upper End of the Cell which is fallen down and broke in half, is, according to Dr. *Hales*, 25 Feet in Length, 7 Feet in Breadth, and at a Medium 3 ½ Feet in Thickneſs, and amounts to 612 Cubic Feet: but Dr. *Stukeley* makes the Dimenſions of this Stone ſtill larger, and ſuppoſes that it weighs above 40 Tons, and requires above 140 Oxen to draw it ; yet this is not the heavieſt Stone at the Place.

Great Injury has been done to theſe Stones by the unaccountable Folly of Mankind in breaking Pieces off with great Hammers ; a Practice which aroſe from the ſilly Notion of theſe Stones being factitious ; but Dr. *Stuckeley* thinks it would be a greater Wonder to make them by Art, than to carry them 16 Miles by Art and Strength ; and thoſe People muſt be inexcuſable who deface the Monument for ſo trifling a Conſideration. Others think, that all the Wonder of the Work conſiſts in the Difficulty of counting the Stones, and in this Employment Numbers of daily Viſitants are conſtantly employed.

Rude as the Work ſeems, there is not a Stone here which has not felt more or leſs, both the Axe and Chiſel of the Workmen, and indeed the Bulk of the conſtituent Parts is ſo very great, that the Mortoiſes and Tenons muſt have been made with great Exactneſs ; theſe are formed with great Simplicity. The upright Stones are made to diminiſh a little every Way ; by which Means the Impoſts project no leſs than 2 Feet 7 Inches, which is very conſiderable in a Height of 18. On the Top of each of the upright Stones is a Tenon, reſembling rather Half an Egg than an Hemiſphere, which is 10 Inches and an Half in Diameter, and made exactly to fit the Mortoiſes made in the Impoſts. On the Outſide, the Impoſts are rounded a little to humour the Circle ; but within they are ſtrait and make a Polygon of 30 Sides, which, without injuring the Beauty of the Work, adds to the Strength of the whole. The Height of the Uprights and Impoſts is ten Cubits and a Half ; the Uprights 9 Cubits, and the Impoſts 1 ½.

Of this outer Circle, which, in its Perfection conſiſted of 60 Stones, 30 Uprights, and 30 Impoſts, there are 17 Uprights left ſtanding ; 11 of which remain continuous by the grand Entrance, which is ſomething wider than the reſt ; with five Impoſts

posts upon them. One Upright at the Back of the Temple, or on the South-West, leans upon a Stone of the inner Circle: There are six others lying upon the Ground, whole or in Pieces. So that 24 out of 30 are still there. There is only one Impost more in its proper Place, and two lying upon the Ground; so that 22 are carried off.

Somewhat more than 8 Feet from the Inside of this exterior Circle, is another of 40 smaller Stones without any Imposts, which, with the outer Circle, form, as it were, a circular Portico. These are a Cubit thick, and four Cubits and an Half in Height, being every Way the Half of the outer Uprights. Of these there are only 19 left; of which 11 only are standing; five in one Place standing contiguous, three in another, and two in another. The Walk, between these two Circles, which was 300 Feet in Circumference, must have had a very fine Effect.

But, besides this outer Portico, there is an inner one, which originally composed about two Thirds of an Oval; the outer Parts of which is formed of certain Compages of Stones, which Dr *Stukeley* calls *Trilithons*, because each of these Compages is formed of two upright Stones, with an Impost at Top. The Stones, of which these *Trilithons* are composed, are really stupendous; their Height, Breadth, and Thickness are enormous; and cannot fail of filling the Beholder with Surprise. Each *Trilithon* stands by itself, independent of its Neighbour, not as the Uprights and Imposts of the outer Circle, linked together by the Imposts carried quite round. The Breadth of a Stone at Bottom is seven Feet and an Half, the two Stones therefore amount to 15 Feet; and there is a Cubit, or 20 $\frac{4}{5}$ Inches between them, making on the whole near 17 Feet: But these Stones diminish very much towards the Top, and were probably so formed with a Design to take off from their Weight, and render them in a less Degree top-heavy. They rise in Height and Beauty of the Stones from the lower End on each Side next the principal Entrance, to the upper End. That is, the two hithermost *Trilithons* on the right and left, are exceeded in Height, by the two next in Order, and these are exceeded by the *Trilithon* behind the Altar, at the upper End. These *Trilithons* are upon a Medium 20 Feet high: Their Heights

O 2

respecpectively are 13 Cubits, 14 Cubits, and 15 Cubits; but the Imposts on the Top are all of the same Size. There are manifestly 5 of the *Trilithons* remaining, of which 3 are entire, and though 2 are in some Measure ruined, the Stones remain in Sight.

On the Inside of this Oval is a lesser Oval of 19 Stones of somewhat of a pyramidical Form, these are two Feet 6 Inches in Breadth, one Foot and an Half thick, and upon a Medium 8 Feet high, they rising in Height, as they approach the upper End of this Inclosure. Of these there are only 6 Stones remaining upright.

The Space within this inward Inclosure, has been called the *Adytum*, or the *Sanctum Sanctorum*, which, it is supposed, was only entered by the Druids, or *British* Priests, who offered their Sacrifices on the Altar at the upper End. This Altar is a Kind of blue coarse Marble 20 Inches thick, 4 Feet broad, and, according to Mr. Webb, 16 Feet in Length.

All the Stones added together, with which this whole Temple was built, make just 140. This is the Solution of the mighty Problem, that has so much perplexed the Vulgar.

We shall only add, that the most early Method of building Temples was to make them open at Top ; and this is a Proof of the prodigious Antiquity of this Fabric. And it must be owned, that they who had a Notion, that it was degrading the Deity to pretend to confine him within a limited Space, could not easily invent a grander Design for sacred Purposes, nor execute it in a more magnificent Manner. Here Space indeed is marked out, and defined; but with the utmost Freedom. Here the Presence of the Deity is intimated, but not bounded. " And here the Variety and Harmony of four differing Circles " presents itself continually new, every Step we take, with " opening and closing Light and Shade. Which Way soever " we look, Art and Nature make a Composition of their high- " est Gusto, create a pleasing Astonishment very apposite to sa- " cred Places." *

At

* To this Account which Dr. *Stukely* gives of *Stonehenge*, I shall take the Liberty of subjoining a few Remarks, and shall, in the first Place, observe, That the Doctor has said as much as the Nature of Things will allow (if not more) in the Defence of the Notion he has ad-

At a small Distance to the East of *Stonehenge* is situated *Ambresbury*, near the *Avon*, which had its Name from *Ambrosius Aurelianus*, who in the Declension of the *Roman* Empire, assumed the Government of *Britain*. This Town, it is said, is remarkable for a little Fish, taken in the River, called a *Loach*, which Travellers, and particularly the Sportsmen, who resort hither

advanced, concerning the Origin of this wonderful Piece of Antiquity, and the Nature of the Stones of which it consists. But as to the Original of *Stonehenge* it does not appear from all that he has said, that it was certainly a finished Temple at first, or ever built by the *Druids*, and that we think he has not so much as made it probable that the Stones which compose it are natural or not factitious.

For first, we cannot see any Reason to suppose that this Temple was ever complete or finished, because it is confessed that a great Number of Stones, and many of the largest Size, are now wanting, and no where to be found, which must be supposed to have been there used, when the Temple was compleated. The prodigious Labour, Time and Expence, imployed in demolishing such a Structure, to answer no End at the same Time, make it more than probable, that it was never once completed; but what is still a greater Proof of this is, that those Stones which are now wanting, must still have been in Being, and would have been seen or found at no great Distance from the Place; for though the Reasons alledged for bringing them from *Marlborough Downs* to this Place, be slender enough, yet none at all can be assigned, why, when this Temple was destroyed, they should carry those Stones so far away, as to be utterly lost; for there is but one to be found within many Miles of the Place, and it is highly probable, that one was never at *Stonehenge*. If it was possible for them to carry those prodigious Stones to any Distance, they surely would not have taken the fruitless Pains of burying them so deep under Ground as never since to have been discovered, and it is very certain they could not love Labour so well as to knock them all to Pieces, and yet something of this Kind they must have done, or the Number of Stones first employed, must always afterwards have been found on the Spot, but at present of the 30 upright Stones, which made the outer Circle, there are only 24 left, and of the 30 Imposts, or top Stones, there are only eight left; so that out of 60 Stones, which made this grand Circle, there are nearly one half, *viz.* 28 missing, or, in the Doctor's own Words, *carried away by rude and sacrilegious Hands for other Uses*. Such Rudeness, such Sacrilege as this, may easily be forgiven in those poor thievish Miscreants, who despoiled this famous Temple for the Sake of Labour only.

We shall say nothing here, concerning the Geometry originally employed, in laying out the Ground-plot or Plan of *Stonehenge*; the two exact Circles of the outer Part, and the two perfect Ellipses on the inner Part (in the Focus of which the Altar-stone is supposed to be placed), one sees so little of, at present, in a general View of

Stone-

140

hither for the Sake of Hunting on the neighbouring Downs, put into a Glafs of Sack, and fwallow alive.

Stonehenge upon the Spot, that no one poffeffed of a fmall Degree of Skill in the antient *Druid* Architecture, would ever have fufpected any fuch Thing.

That this Temple was certainly built by the *Druids*, is (after all the Doctor has faid) far from being a Point clearly and fairly proved: The Hiftory of the *Druids*, and of all the antient dark Times in which they lived, is fo very imperfect as to prove nothing; there is no credible Account, of their being a People of fuch extraordinary Genius, Prowefs and Skill that fhall enable them to perform fuch wonderful Feats in Mechanics, as not only would foil all the Mathematicians in *Britain*, but even in *Europe*, or the World itfelf, in this very learned and improved Age. All that *Cæfar* fays of this antient People, will avail us little towards proving that they had any geometrical or architectonic Skill at all, much lefs fuperior to that of all Ages fince. As to the Meafures ufed in conftructing the Work being a Cubit, it is not clear (fuppofing that true) that ever the *Druids* built this Temple, or that ever they were a *Phænician* Colony; for thefe Stones cannot be meafured by the *Hebrew* Cubit, without Fractions, as being very irregular in every Part, nothing can be more common than Fractions in the Meafurement of the Parts of any Building, therefore the Argument of the Meafures *falling into Fractions*, does not prove that the Architects were of one Nation rather than another, and therefore *Inigo Jones* (the celebrated Architect of our Age) might as well fuppofe it a Work of the *Romans*, and of the *Tufcan Order*, as that it was erected by the *Druids*, and of no Order at all ; the *Romans*, it is well known, were a People of great Skill in Mechanics, and always inured to Works of a very extraordinary Nature ; if they had built this Temple it had been no Wonder, their Skill in Mechanics would have accounted for it, in Part, that is to fay, for all that was done at *Stonehenge* on the Spot; for as to what relates to bringing the Stones thither from any Diftance, is what we fhall next proceed to fhew was a Tafk too mighty for even themfelves to take, with all their Power and Skill.

There has been always two Opinions refpecting the Nature of thefe Stones, the firft is, that they are *natural*; the other is, that they are *factitious*, or made by Art ; our learned Antiquarian efpoufes the firft or common Opinion, and roundly afferts, *That the Stones of which* Stonehenge *is compofed, beyond all Controverfy, came from thofe called* Grey-Weathers, *upon* Marlborough Downs, *which is* 15 *or* 16 *Miles off*. But, by the Doctor's Leave, this is a Matter not quite beyond all Controverfy, for tho' he is pleafed to fay, in another Place, *That the Stones of the* Grey Weathers *lay on the Surface of the Ground, in infinite Numbers,*

and

and of full Dimenfions; yet I, who have often furveyed thefe Stones, never obferved any fuch Thing as a Stone among them that bore any Refemblance to thofe at Stonehenge, efpecially in Regard of their Bulk: There is no Stone among the Grey Weathers, that I could ever obferve, fo large as to equal in Bulk any of the leffer Sort at Stonehenge, much lefs is it likely there was ever any appeared in former Times, much larger than the largeft in that wonderous Pile, for when firft taken out of the Earth they muft needs have been much larger, fince a great deal muft have been hewn and chifeled away to bring them to their prefent Form. And we fhall venture to fay, that Stones in the Ground are larger now than they were 3000 Years ago, for that they grow from Age to Age bigger and bigger, is at leaft a Piece of Philofophy as well grounded, (and can be better proved by Experiments) *than that the Grey Weathers on* Marlborough Downs, *has lain there ever fince the Creation, and were thrown out to the Surface of the Fluid Globe when its Rotation was firft impreffed.*

We muft farther obferve, that neither Dr. *Stukeley*, nor any other Author upon the Subject, has given any plaufible or fatisfactory Account of the Reafons, why the Place where *Stonehenge* now ftands, fhould be made choice of, rather than *Marlborough Downs*, fince Stones might there have been had with fmall Expence and Trouble, and as it is a much higher Situation, one would be induced to think it a more proper Place for the Purpofes of religious Worfhip; fince it is well known, the antient eaftern Idolaters always built their Temples and Altars upon high Places. But if *Salisbury Plain* muft be chofe, let us next confider which will be the greateft *Wonder*, *to make them by Art*, *or to carry them* 16 *Miles by Art and Strength.* The Doctor is pleafed to call the Notion of their being factitious a *filly one*; but filly as it is, it is my Opinion, when all Things are confidered, we fhall find it more for our Credit to be, in this Cafe, a little filly, than over-wife; we have at leaft a Poffibility, and fome Degree of Probability, that they were made by Art, but it will require too much Underftanding for People in common to conceive, that it is poffible, or even probable, they fhould be brought from *Marlborough Downs*, or wrought into their prefent Forms by Art.

That it is poffible they might be made by Art, no Man can difpute, who confiders, that the Subftance of common Stones, reduced to Powder and mixed with proper Ingredients, will compofe a Subftance that fhall appear like Stone, and at the fame Time be harder and heavier; and a Perfon poffeffed of this Art, to a furprizing Degree, was, a few Years ago, well known in *England*, and gave fuch Proof of his Skill this Way, as prevented his getting a Patent for practifing his Art, left *Mafonry* and other Trades
fhould

142

should be hurt by it. Of this Sort the Stones at *Stonehenge* appear to me; they seem to the Eye to be different from common Stone, and when I found I was obliged with a Hammer to Labour hard three Quarters of an Hour to get but one Ounce and half, I was fully convinced, their Hardness, or Fixity, by much exceeded that of common Stone. I was also farther assured by taking the specific Gravity of the Pieces, which I found to be 2.6 at a Mean; whereas that of Stone, in general, is not more than 2.5, that there was some Reason also on this Account to think they were factitious or made by Art. Why this Practice, which is necessary to give us an Insight into the Nature of the Stone, should be called a trifling *Fancy*, is a little strange; and will, we presume, by a very few People, be thought an Argument of *vulgar Incogitancy*.

But now let us reflect what Kind of Cogitancy we must imply to bring these Stones from *Marlborough Downs*, &c. By the Doctor's own Account some Stones are at least 40 Tons, and require more than 140 Oxen to draw one of them in their present Form, and we may reasonably suppose that they were much larger before they were wrought, and therefore required a greater Strength to draw them. It appears also that the Number of Stones to compleat the Temple must be 140: Now let any one confider, how immence a Labour it must be to cut and hew those very large Stones into their present Form and Figure; and at the same Time there is not the least Appearance of an Axe or Chisel upon them; and lastly, how great the Strength, the Time, and Art, must be, to carry them at so great a Distance; to conceive all these Things, I say, but bearly possible, requires a Stretch of Thought, beyond vulgar Cogitation indeed! Nay, 'tis but sometimes that the Doctor himself is able to understand and account for such a Prodigy of Art; for when Mr. *Webb* insisted upon there being six Trilithons, and five only remaining, the Doctor employs a merry Vein upon him, and says, that he supposes one Trilithon entirely gone: But, says the Doctor, there is no Cavity in the Earth, no Stump or Fragment visible, nor is it easy to imagine how three Stones of so vast a Bulk could have been clean carried away either whole or in Pieces: — And a little after, — What has been thrown down and broke remains upon the Spot, but this Trilithon in Dispute must needs have been spirited away, by nothing less than *Merlin's* Magic, which erected it, as fabled by the Monks. ——— Here we may see that our Author thinks it an impossible Task, for one Trilithon to be carried away, when five others, and all the rest of the Monument, were at first brought hither without employing any Spirits, or *Merlin's* Dæmons for that Purpose; but it is Time to drop a Subject where there is so little room for a Dispute upon the Principles of common Reason and Experiments.

5.
Observations on the writings of William Lisle Bowles

Rodney Legg extracts some observations by Thomas William Wake Smart, M.D. on the writings of William Lisle Bowles

THE COPY of William Lisle Bowles's *Dissertation on the Celtic Deity Teutates*, published in 1828, that was owned by the Dorset antiquary Thomas William Wake Smart is heavily annotated. Wake Smart was the author in 1841 of the *Chronicle of Cranborne* and his notes in the Bowles's volume throw light on the mid-Victorian reappraisal of Stonehenge and the Wessex antiquities.

It was in the 1860s that the concept of the three prehistoric periods was introduced, and Wake Smart had no hesitation in assigning Stonehenge to the central phase: "The Trilithons are hewn stones, and have the tenon and mortice evidence of metallic tools: in every respect greatly inferior in antiquity to Avebury. Stonehenge belongs to the Bronze Age."

He doubted Lisle Bowles's suggestion that the dispersion of the Egyptians, westwards in the reign of Pharaoh Hophni, might have carried their doctrines "even to the isles of the sea," and pointed out: "The temples of Avebury are probably of a much higher antiquity than B.C. 600."

The Bowles argument was taken a stage further: "The vast pile, in the first place, I consider as sacred to that great instructor, symbolised and worshipped in Egypt, who unfolded the heavens and brought intelligence of one infinite god and of eternal life to man; which knowledge, in remote ages, was communicated to the Celtic Druids by the Phoenicians. The inner circles represent, severally, the months of the year, the days, and the hours, included in the great circles of eternity, stretching on each side in the form of the 'serpent', the well known emblem, both of the course of the stars and of restoration and immortality...."

147

"I believe all this to be 'bosh'," Wake Smart writes. "It symbolised the sun, or rather the apparent course of the sun. It is simply conjectural to say that the Druidical religion was brought to Britain by the Phoenicians. We have no evidence to show that they came to the shores of Britain for any purpose but trade. The Egyptians, and the Celts, may have got their religious knowledge from a common primaeval source." 'Bosh,' a Turkish word for worthless opinion, came into use in Britain in the 1860s.

Bowles mentions the discovery of a flint arrowhead with a bronze dagger beside it in a grave near Woodyates Inn, Dorset. He remarks that it is utterly incredible for brass to be manufactured "by him who had not knowledge to discover or skill to form his arrow's point out of other materials than a flint of the Downs."

Wake Smart writes: "Simply a tumulus of the 'Bronze era'. There can be no doubt that bronze weapons were manufactured in Britain, though not to such an extent as to be of general use, or to supersede the use of flint entirely. The knowledge of metallurgy probably came from Gaul."

He gives the location of the barrow, which Sir Richard Colt Hoare had opened in a thunderstorm, and Bowles used as the inspiration for his verse of *The Celtic Warrior's Grave*. Wake Smart records: "My father and mother, and Mr and Mrs Stillingfleet were present. The tumulus was situated on Woodyates Down, by the side of the Turnpike road, not far from the XI milestone." This milestone (Blandford 11, Sarum 11) is in Pentridge parish at the north end of Oakley Down, at SU 021176.

Wake Smart rejects Bowles's footnote claim that the Roman road across Cranborne Chase "deviates from its right line, as in respect to the dead":

"This is certainly not correct — for the Via Iceniana here cuts through the side of one of the sacred enclosures, or Druid barrows, so called by Hoare."

As evidence of "the Phoenicians being the founders of the Druidical discipline in Britain," Bowles includes a drawing of a Tyrian coin. It shows an oak tree, with an "anointed rocks" caption beneath two stone pillars of Hercules, and Bowles writes: "Let the reader remember the Monkish tradition of Ambrosius! The exact likeness of these pillars, on this coin, to the stones of Stonehenge, the Ambrosiae Petrae; and if he does not think the origin of Ambrosebury, or Amesbury, was derived from the Ambrosiae Petrae, or anointed stones of the Tyrian colonists, he will think the coincidence most remarkable."

Wake Smart refuses to accept the evidence. "Is this coin authentic?" he asks. "Where is it to be seen? Probably 'W.A. Miles invenit'!"

There is a second reference to the coin and here Wake Smart adds: "Most probably one of the inventions of William Augustus Miles! A gentleman whom I knew well — very visionary, very clever!"

Miles had suggested there had been a Phoenician colony on the Dorset coast at Hambury Tout, Lulworth Cove. He had also written on the shale 'coins' found in the Isle of Purbeck, and this leads Wake Smart to make what seems to be the earliest realisation of their true origins: "The Kimmeridge 'coal money' is most probably of Roman manufacture, being the refuse of the lathe in turning rings."

William Augustus Miles was a political pamphleteer, whose antiquarian researches were carried out for leisure. He retired to Dorset in 1803, to a house on Brownsea Island in Poole Harbour, lent him by his friend Charles Sturt. Miles died in Paris at the age of 64 on 25 April 1817, having been in the country a year — including a month's stay with Lafayette — collecting material for a history of the French revolution.

Regarding the Cerne Giant, and its supposed ancient name, Helith, Wake Smart writes: "There is a Hel-well at Cerne." This was a spring. But he is dismissive of attempts to credit the Dorset hill figure with any great age: "Se non è vero è ben trorato. In my humble opinion the Cerne Giant, whose acquaintance I made many years ago when a pupil with the Revd. John Davis of Cerne, was a rustic or a monkish work of the Middle Ages, suggested by some popular legend of that day which abounded in tales of imaginary Giants. Whether such legends were allusive to ancient modes of worship is another question."

6.
Shall Stonehenge Go?

Thomas Hardy was fascinated with antiquities and brought Stonehenge into the climax of *Tess of the d'Urbervilles*. He was enraged when he heard that the monument might be crated up and re-erected in America. This report by "Our Special Correspondent" appeared on page three of the *Daily Chronicle* on 24 August 1899. The by-line might indicate authorship by a freelance or staff reporter on a local weekly paper, but Hardy was shy of the press and it is known that this interview with James Milne was conducted postally. The substance of the report was provided by Hardy in a five page draft, a rough of which is preserved in the Howard Bliss collection. The reporter was a *Chronicle* staff man who rounded it off convincingly with observations on the weather and other atmospheric touches. The questions had been sent to Hardy, and for clarity they are set here in *italics*. Note that Hardy, for all his sensitivity, suggested that the monument should be surrounded by plantations

YESTERDAY I went down into Wessex to ask Mr. Thomas Hardy what he thought about Stonehenge. That mysterious relic belongs to all England, but is the hub of olden Wessex.

As his friends know, the great novelist of Wessex is most timorous of appearing in any public way, except through his writings. Had I sallied south to lionise Mr Hardy himself I should, almost surely, have had no luck. It was different to have for my subject Stonehenge – Stonehenge in the market.

"On such an occasion," Mr Hardy admitted, "one may fairly enough be called upon to speak, only I am not entitled to give any authoritative opinion in regard to Stonehenge and its future, as I have no more knowledge of the monument than is common to, or obtainable by anybody who chooses to visit it."

Well, to say nothing more, Mr Hardy added to its fame when he wrote that fine scene in *Tess of the d'Urbervilles*. He made special visits to Stonehenge to get his lights for the chapter; and, broadly, to use his own homely phrase, he lives within a bicycle ride of it. At Max Gate, his house on a brow of ground overlooking Dorchester, I found him in cycling costume. It was a badge of the good health which shone in his face and found expression in his alert walk as he led the way across his garden to a summerhouse.

"Here," he said, "we have both shade and the open air, two grateful things." The sun burned hot – had done so all the road from London, though indeed you whirled through the pines, by stretches of sea, past beds of red heather, all giving freshness to the day. Wessex was drowsy under the sun's rays, but looking out upon it Mr Hardy was all eagerness for its unique Stonehenge.

"The intimation that the relic is for sale," he went on, "has quite taken me by surprise. That is the more so because I used to hear that the late Sir Edmund Antrobus would not have a stone turned, even for research, lest the monument might by any chance be injured. I believe that a well-known antiquarian asked him for permission to conduct two days' digging in the vicinity of the relic, but was refused, for the reason I have mentioned."

"Of course, the object of the inquiry would have been to settle, if that were possible, the history of Stonehenge?"

"Just so, there are many theories, but the smallest amount of evidence, yielded by remains which might be discovered, would be most valuable. Now, if the statements which have appeared in the papers are to be accepted, we practically have Stonehenge put up for auction to any bidder at home or abroad. Frankly, I cannot realise the possibility of Stonehenge being carted out of the country, say, by the rich American who is rumored to have

154

made an offer for it. No, no; nobody would think of that in any sort of circumstances."

"You feel that Stonehenge, while it may be private property, is nevertheless, and above all, a national possession?"

"Yes; and here a general statement may be made. A nation like our own ought to have what may be called a final guardianship over any monument or relic which is of value to it as a page of history, even though the hieroglyphics of such a monument or relic cannot be deciphered as yet. I don't know how this is to be brought about – it is not for myself to make any suggestion – but that the thing is desirable and right there cannot, I fancy, be two opinions. In fact, we assume that the owner of property on which there happens to be a national relic, is in the larger sense the custodian for the nation of that relic. It is possible to conceive circumstances wherein this might be an individual hardship, only there it is. But to return, it is evident that the case of Stonehenge will not wait, and therefore has to be treated by itself."

"And in your view what should be done?"

"I assume that in all events Stonehenge must remain the wonder of Salisbury Plain, and of England, which it has been for so many centuries – a sacred possession. Why, merely give two thoughts to the bare idea of anything else. Suppose, for argument's sake – nothing more – that you carry the stones to America and re-erect them there. What happens? They lose all interest, because they would not form Stonehenge; and the same with the Stonehenge which was left. The relics being gone the associations of the place would be broken, all the sentiments would have evaporated. Altogether, it would be as if King Solomon had cut the child in two, leaving no child at all."

"We return to the line for the people and for Government?"

"Emphatically Stonehenge should be purchased by the nation, since apparently it is to be sold. More, I welcome the chance, because I have never liked the idea of its being private property. The essential condition is that it should be obtainable for a fair price, such as might be agreed upon after due investigation. Inquiry and arbitration – that is what I would suggest; and until then there is little use in speaking of figures. It seems to me, however, that there is no call for the nation to purchase all the land that has been offered along with Stonehenge. A certain area – shall we put it at 2,000 acres? – must be bought as securing control of the surroundings of the monument. It derives much from its site – the freedom, the feeling of Salisbury Plain – and that element must be safeguarded. It would never do for somebody to get a plot of ground near by, and on it, given the humour, erect a building."

"Your advice is this – that the nation should buy Stonehenge and its immediate surroundings, paying a fair price, and no more, as arbitration might fix."

"That's it, the last word always being the supremacy of the nation. It ought to be possible to name a price which any reasonable man would be willing to accept. What should next be done, or if anything else should be done, is a more difficult question."

"You mean the condition of the ruins and the best means of preserving them?"

"What strikes a visitor accustomed to observe the effect of years and weather on ruins so exposed as these, is that the dilapidation in progress is not so insignificant as may be cursorily imagined. Wet weather and frost are, as all know, the destructive factors in the case, and to the best of my recollection it is on the south-west face of the ruin that decay goes on most rapidly. On this south-west side time nibbles year after year, and it is only owing to the shelter afforded by the south-west walls to the rest of the structure, that any of the columns are erect – all these being the ones to the north-east. Indeed, to those persons who have had the misfortune to be on Salisbury Plain in a piercing downpour, and have noticed, or rather have felt, how the drops pass into them like arrows, it is a matter of wonder that the erection has stood so long."

"Is the wet the chief enemy?"

"Well, you see, apart from the effect of the water on the stones themselves, they are gradually undermined by the trickling down of the rain they intercept, forming pools on the ground, so that the foundation sinks on the wettest side till the stone topples over. There are only three architraves now remaining supported on their proper pillars, and as these decline the architraves will slip off. The only way of protecting the ruin from driving rains which will ultimately abrade and overthrow them, would be by a belt of plantations."

"But the landscape?"

"Yes, against such planting there is to be urged that most people consider the gaunt nakedness of its situation to be a great part of the solemnity and fascination of Stonehenge. It is by no means certain, however, that the country immediately round it was originally bare and open on all sides, and if it were enclosed by a wood approaching no nearer than, say, ten chains to the bank of earth surrounding the stone circle, the force of these disastrous winds and rains would be broken by the trees, and the duration of the ruin lengthened far beyond its possible duration now. As cultivation and agricultural buildings have latterly advanced over the plain, till they are quite near the spot and interfere with its loneliness, the objection to such planting would be less in that the trees would shut out these incongruities."

"You, who know Stonehenge intimately, have perhaps got impressions there which don't occur to the mere visitor?"

"The size of the whole structure is considerably dwarfed to the eye by the openness of the place, as with all such erections, and a strong light detracts from its impressiveness. In the brilliant noonday sunlight, in which most visitors repair thither, and surrounded by bicycles and sandwich papers, the scene is not to my mind attractive, but garish and depressing. In dull, threatening weather, however, and in the dusk of the evening its charm is indescribable. On a day of heavy cloud the sky seems almost to form a natural roof touching the pillars, and colours are revealed on the surfaces of the stones whose presence would not be suspected on a fine day. And if a gale of wind is blowing the strange musical hum emitted by Stonehenge can never be forgotten. To say that on moonlight nights it is at its finest is a commonplace."

"Have you any personal opinion as to the probable

origin of Stonehenge?"

"All one can say is that the building was probably erected after the barrow period of interment in these islands, from the fact that one or two barrows seem to have been interfered with in its construction. The problem of the purpose and date of Stonehenge could possibly be narrowed down from its present vagueness, if not settled, by a few days' excavation near the spot. This, if done at all, should be carried out under the strictest supervision. Personally I confess to a liking for the state of dim conjecture in which we stand with regard to its history."

But Mr Hardy wants no "dim conjecture" as to the future of Stonehenge.

7.
How Stonehenge became desecrated and vulgarised by barbed-wire

Lord Eversley, the founder in 1865 of Britain's first countryside pressure group, the Commons Preservation Society, led the losing battle to uphold the right of free public access to Stonehenge. "Let us fence out the hateful, vulgar public," seemed to be the view of the judiciary. This account of that struggle was written in 1910

STONEHENGE is well recognised as the most imposing and interesting of all the prehistoric remains in this country. The circle of stones stands in the midst of a vast expanse of the Wiltshire Downs, about seven miles from Salisbury. It owed, till lately, much of its solemnity to its weird solitude in the adjoining plain. It is surrounded by a vallum, in which there are three or four gaps, and through which well-defined and long-worn tracks or roadways (not made roads) give access to the inner circle of stones. These roadways cross the Downs for long distances, and it is certain that for centuries they have been used by great numbers of people visiting the monument originally for some religious purpose, but later, on account of its historic and antiquarian interest.

Of recent years carriages from Salisbury, in great numbers, have conveyed visitors by one of these tracks through the vallum to the stones, returning by another opening of the vallum; thus making a continuous round or track through another route, not abruptly ending at the stones. Another track was a through route from Salisbury to Durrington, passing through the vallum. It was much used a few years ago by carts conveying coal and farm produce, but since the opening of the station at Amesbury, has been less frequented. No one had ever been forbidden the use of these tracks.

On June 20th in every year, from time immemorial, it had been the custom of many hundreds of persons to assemble at Stonehenge, at sunrise, in order to watch the first rays of the rising sun strike the sacrificial stone in a line with the centre of the circle of stones. This seems to have been an ancient custom, having its origin probably in the worship of the sun.

In 1882, when at the head of the Office of Works, after passing the Ancient Monuments Act, I directed the General Augustus Pitt Rivers, whom I had appointed Inspector under it, to communicate with Sir Edmund Antrobus, the then owner of the land on which Stonehenge stands, and to suggest to him the expediency of placing the monument under the protection of the Act. The owner declined to do this. He resented any suggestion that he was neglectful of his duty to protect the monument from injury, or that it was necessary for the Government to intervene for that purpose.

Later, in 1894, when I was again at the head of the same department, there was some correspondence in the press complaining that injury was being done to the stones by visitors or tramps. On my writing to Sir E. Antrobus on the subject, he denied in the most positive terms that any injury had been done. The scribbling of names complained of, he said, was only on the moss, and did not injure the surface of the stones. He referred to a proposal for fencing the monument, but only to repudiate it, and to suggest the probability that, if effected, an indignant public might act as the London public did in regard to the railings of Hyde Park, when the claim to hold meetings there was interfered with. He protested against a proposal that a policeman's hut should be erected near the monument. The whole tenor of the letter was that he considered himself as holding the monument in trust for the public, and that he recognised their right of access to it. In the course of the suit, his son, the present owner, stated that he had suggested to his father the expediency of blocking up the ways leading to the monument, but his father had refused to do so.

The late Sir Edmund Antrobus died in 1899. His son, also Sir Edmund Antrobus, the present owner, on coming into possession of the property, appeared to value the monument as a means of extorting money for its purchase from the public. He sent his agent, Mr. Squarey, to the Chancellor of the Exchequer, Sir M. Hicks-Beach, with an offer to sell to the Government the monument, with 1,200 acres of downland adjoining it for the sum of £125,000, but with the reservation that the rights of grazing and sporting over the land were to remain vested in him. The sum asked was very little short of the price which his grandfather had given for the whole estate of 4,000 acres constituting the manor, at a time when the value of land in Wiltshire was double what it now is.

When the Chancellor refused to entertain the purchase at such a price, Mr. Squarey suggested that the owner might be persuaded to sell the stones to some American millionaire, who would ship them across the Atlantic. The Chancellor very properly replied to the threat, that if the attempt were made to remove the Stones, he would send a regiment of soldiers to prevent it. A communiqué of the same kind, coupled with the same threat was made to *The Times* by a writer who described himself as a friend of the owner.

In 1901, it was feared that the establishment of a military camp on Salisbury Plain might lead to damage being done to the monument. Some communication was made to the owner on the subject by the Society of Antiquaries, and although it was quite certain that no injury had been effected, Sir E. Antrobus, with their approval, erected a substantial and unsightly barbed-wire fence round the monument, enclosing a few acres. A hut was erected at the entrance to this enclosure, and an entrance fee of one shilling a head was charged to visitors.

The fence cut through the vallum in two places, leaving outside the enclosure a considerable part of the vallum, together with a detached stone said to have possessed some special significance in connection with the ancient use of the monument. This line of the fence was necessitated by the existence of an admitted public highway through the vallum, which could not be obstructed. As a result of this, the public can by means of this roadway approach within a short distance of the stones on one side, and get a peep at them through the fence, though the monument is marred even more seriously than if the whole vallum had been enclosed.

The erection of this fence has entirely altered the character of the monument. The effect has been to rob it of its peculiar character – a strange relic of the twilight of the world, standing untouched through countless centuries – and to convert it into an antiquarian's specimen. It has lost its solemnity, due to its loneliness in the vast plain. The inhabitants of the district, who cannot afford to pay one shilling a head for entrance, have lost their accustomed right of access to it.

The justification for the charge of entrance money was that Sir E. Antrobus could only, in this way, recoup himself for his outlay on the fence, for the cost of raising the fallen stones, and for the wages of the two custodians who guard the monument and collect the fees.

The erection of this unsightly fence, and the exclusion of the general public by the charge of one shilling a head, roused very strong objections on the part of the people of Salisbury and other surrounding districts, and also on the part of a much wider public, who considered that the monument was desecrated by this treatment. The movement was led in the first instance by Professor Flinders Petrie, the eminent Egyptologist. It was pointed out that if the object of the owner was simply to protect the monument, there was a far simpler and better mode of effecting that purpose, by placing it under the protection of the Government under the Ancient Monuments Act. The effect of this would be to impose upon the Government the obligation of protecting the monument against any injury, while in no way interfering with the rights of the owner over it. At the same time access to it by the public would be secured, without the payment of any charge.

At this point an appeal was made to the Commons Preservation Society for their opinion as to the legality of the fence erected round the monument, interfering as it did with the several undoubted tracks or roadways, which the public had used from time immemorial. If the right of the public to use these tracks, or any one of them could be upheld, neither the fence, as erected, nor any other fence could be maintained, as it would be practically impossible so to fence in the Stones as to prevent full access to them by the public, and yet leave the tracks unobstructed.

The Society, after full inquiry into the facts and the law, determined to contest the legality of the obstructing fence, and raised a guarantee fund by public subscription for the purpose. Much delay arose while negotiations took place between the Wiltshire County Council, the Government and Sir E. Antrobus, for the purchase of the monument. The owner reduced his demands to £50,000, but this was refused by the Chancellor of the Exchequer (the late Mr. Ritchie), as altogether exorbitant. The Society then felt that no course was open to it but to commence legal proceedings.

Before doing so, however, it made two offers to the owner – the one, that if he would remove the fences and place the monument under the protection of the Ancient Monuments Act, it would repay all the expenses he had incurred in raising the fallen stones, and erecting the fences. The other, if he preferred to sell the monument, that it would appeal to the public for £10,000 for the purpose, and a further sum to cover the cost of the fences, and would then hand over the monument to the Government for protection under the Act. Sir E. Antrobus replied that he was willing to sell the monument for not less than £50,000, a sum which he considered of moderate amount in comparison for what was given for ancient Abbeys.

The Society accepted the analogy between Stonehenge and an ancient Abbey, and pointed out that two cases had occurred in recent years where ruined Abbeys of great beauty had been purchased in the public interest, namely Kirkstall Abbey, near Leeds, bought by the Corporation of Leeds, and Tintern Abbey, bought by the Commissioners of Woods and Forests on behalf of the Crown, and that in both cases the price had been £10,000. Sir E. Antrobus made no rejoinder to this.

The suit took the form of an action in the name of the Attorney-General, calling upon the owner to remove the fences which obstructed the public rights-of-way. The relators, or parties to the suit, were Professor Petrie, Sir

John Brunner and myself. The consent of the Attorney-General was no mere formality, but was only given after careful consideration, and upon being satisfied that a question of grave importance to the public was involved, which ought to be brought before the High Courts of Justice.

The case came before Mr. Justice Farwell, now Lord Justice Farwell. It appeared to present itself to him as one in which the owner of the monument had been compelled, as a matter of duty, to erect the fence for its protection. He assumed that damage had already been done to it, though there was no evidence to this effect, and as this was not an issue in the case, the relators could not tender evidence to show that the stones had in no way been injured. He apeared to regard with equanimity the exclusion from the monument of the great bulk of the public. He was evidently under the impression that the vulgar populace had, by their destructive propensities, disqualified themselves as visitors to a place of antiquarian interest.

He quoted the well-known lines of Horace as to the deteriorating habits of succeeding generations of men. He seemed to be inspired by another equally well-known line of the same poet "Odi profanum vulgus et arceo" which may be freely translated "Let us fence out the hateful vulgar public." It was not possible in the proceedings to discuss the alternative method of preserving the monument from injury, by placing it under the protection of the Ancient Monuments Act, or to refer to the negotiations for the sale of the monument to the Government, or to the exorbitant demands of the owner, or to the offer made by the relators. Under these conditions it was not perhaps matter for surprise that the learned judge made every presumption of fact and law against the relators.

With respect to the track from Salisbury to Durrington, the relators called fifteen witnesses, mostly carters, who gave evidence as to the users of the track for fifty years back, with remarkable clearness and evident truthfulness. They were in no way personally interested. Their evidence was set aside by the judge on the ground either that they were persons not likely to be stopped, on their way along the track, by the tenants of the land through which it passed, or that they were untrustworthy, in the sense that they were "illiterate, obviously exaggerating, and inaccurate". He accepted against their cumulative evidence the testimony of a single farmer, tenant for a few recent years of part of the downland on the route of the track, that he had never seen persons use the track except one, and after seeing him five or six times stopped him.

The defendant, Sir E. Antrobus, claimed that he held part of the land, through which the alleged track ran, under a family settlement dating from the year 1826, and that since then no one had been in possession with power to dedicate a right-of-way. He also maintained that a small part of the land had been part of a common, which had been enclosed in the year 1823, and that under the award no mention had been made of this track, and that the tithe map made under the Tithe Apportionment Act gave no indication of the road. It has not been usual to treat inclosure awards or tithe maps as conclusive as to the non-existence of footpaths, especially in the case of open Downland, such as the plain in question. The judge, however, held that both these documents were conclusive on the point – and he further held that, under the family settlement, no one was in a position to dedicate a right-of-way since 1826.

As regards the other important part of the case the right of access to Stonehenge itself by the tracks leading through the vallum to the stones, the judge admitted that two of the ways existed in point of fact, and that the public had long used them, but he expressed the opinion that the whole object of the visitors using these tracks was to see the stones. He said that the tracks entered the vallum but did not cross so as to create a continuous and circuitous way, though all the fly drivers and others in their evidence testified that they were in the habit of going by one track and returning by another. The claim he said was to use tracks which in fact led to nowhere. On this point he laid down in clear and unmistakeable terms that "there cannot be a *prima facie* right for the public to go to a place where the public have no right to be". A public road," he said, "is *prima facie*, a road that leads from one public place to another public place." He admitted, however, that the want of a terminus *ad quem*, was not essential to the legal existence of a public road. It was a question of evidence in each case between the landowner and the public. It was competent to the landowner to execute a deed of dedication or by similar unmistakeable evidence to testify to his intention. He distinguished the case of the Giants' Causeway because in that case the road in question had been "presented" by the Grand Jury in 1824, and had on one occasion been repaired by the public authority.

After a hearing which lasted seven days, the judge upon the above points decided against the relators, and expressed a strong opinion that the suit ought not to have been brought by them – an opinion which must be held to include the Attorney-General who had given his authority for it.

With all respect for the learned judge, the Society, with its long experience in analogous cases, could not accept his opinion, as stated, as a final exposition of the law, nor could they agree that the evidence of a large number of witnesses, not personally interested, should be rejected because they were illiterate. It may be asked why under these circumstances it was not thought well to appeal to a Higher Court. The answer is, that in Mr. Justice Farwell's judgment the questions of law and fact were so mixed up, and with every presumption against the public and in favour of the landowner, that it was almost impossible to disentangle the case, so as to obtain a decision on the purely legal questions of the right of access by the public to a place of interest, and of the presumption of dedication in the case of a footway over land under family settlement.

It was most important that these questions should be raised before a Court of Appeal. But great mischief might be done to the general cause by getting an adverse decision in a case decided by the exclusion of evidence, which would have thrown light on the action of the relators. It was thought better to raise these points in some future case more free from these difficulties. It must be admitted also that the question of costs was a very serious one. The costs of the suit had already been heavy, far beyond the expectation of the relators. The taxed costs of the landowner for which the relators became liable, amounted to no less than £2,250, and those of the relators themselves amounted to £1,650, together nearly £4,000, or £2,500 more than the guarantee fund. The Society's committee found great difficulty in meeting this heavy charge. The prospect of further heavy costs in an appeal to the Lords Justices, with a further possible appeal to the House of Lords, was not an inviting one. But the decision to refrain from appeal was mainly on the grounds of policy already referred to. A large part of the costs of the suit, above the guarantee fund, were met by Sir John Brunner and myself, in unequal proportions, and in part, so far as their personal charges were concerned, by the generous forbearance of the solicitors employed in the case, Messrs. Horne and Birkett.

In this case it must be admitted that the Society was completely defeated in its efforts. The monument of Stonehenge has been desecrated and vulgarised by the erection round it of the barbed-wire fencing; and the great majority of the public, who cannot afford to pay one shilling a head [*equivalent in terms of average weekly wages to £5.00 in 1982*] for entrance to the enclosure, have been permanently excluded. We may doubt whether in any other country in Europe such treatment of a great historical and national monument would be permitted.

8.
Stonehenge, public but untouchable

Rodney Legg rounds off the collection
by taking up Robert Gay's incitement
to shoot his bolt — he did so
in 1980 when the public was
forbidden to approach the monument

THE FENCING of Stonehenge in May 1901 is described by R. J. C. Atkinson in his *Stonehenge* (1956) as "an action which though sensible and long overdue aroused a storm of protest which it is difficult to understand today; it was even proposed by the objectors to test the legality of this proceeding by a law-suit". Well, Mr Atkinson, as the preceding section shows, they went ahead in fact and did just that! It might further be protested that there was nothing illogical in this reaction. The fencing was an offence against the ancient custom of free public access to the monument, which seems to have been built as a temple of the people.

It was regarded in 1901 as outrageous that these rights should be replaced by an exorbitant ticket charge. Shamefully the case fell to an odious judge. "Pour être juge il ne suffit pas être bête." To be a judge, it is not sufficient to be a fool. Perhaps not, but it helps. Lord Eversley should have taken his case to appeal, but it would have been agony enough marshalling the Commons Preservation Society for the first bout of litigation. I do sympathise with him there, as I am the treasurer of that same society today, itself a relic and at times even a dinosaur, though it survives as Britain's oldest countryside amenity group.

Once the monument had fallen into bureaucracy it was inevitable that other controls would follow. They led in time to a sunken car-park, sales kiosk, and an underpass typical of international travel, with lift-style gates that concertina shut. There is a story that the subway was commissioned for the Victoria Line on London's under-

173

ground. In the late 1970's the Environment Department finally achieved the separation of Stonehenge from its audience. There would be fences inside the fencing. Stonehenge is now reserved for the archaeologists, or a privileged clique amongst them who have access to the right channels (presently 01-212-5116, "requests for facilities should be addressed to Mrs Patricia Behr").

Like the buffalo on the last American plains, people herd under the watchful eyes of the state guards. Custodians are uniformed but not yet armed, or perhaps they are by now.

The weight of cameras, carried through the subway daily must make the place worthy of a muggers' convention.

A question arises. Why has the monument been taken away from its public? I think there must be contingency arrangements in the event of a 21-day run-up to nuclear war – when all our art treasures are to be taken underground – that Stonehenge is also to be removed to safety. I speculate that this has already happened, that a Norad computer failure triggered the final alarm, and that Stonehenge was packed-off one night into the bowels of Coombe Down quarries at Bath.

Imagine Whitehall, pace Richard Crossman, though in this case Michael Heseltine would have to be the relevant Secretary of State:

"Now we have it there, Minister, it would hardly be worth the risk to the monument bringing it out, and perhaps one day having to dismantle it again," the permanent secretary suggests. "After all, you wouldn't appreciate the press ringing up to ask why Stonehenge has broken down on a bypass at Devizes. It is not as if anyone has objected to the replica."

"That's because your people won't let anyone near enough to touch it!" (Expressed to a mild display of ministerial table thumping.)

"That's unfair, Minister, we let an author through last July. The custodians took the precaution of establishing that he was unable to read the official guide without glasses."

"If there's more than an inch of rain the stones start

floating off the ground. Surely someone's going to notice?"

"The difficulties have been alleviated since the department authorised a smoke-screen facility. Quite a number of visitors have remarked that they find the mist very atmospheric."

If such a conversation has not taken place then there must be another explanation for the exclusion of the public. It cannot be the stones themselves. For Wiltshire sarsen is two-and-a-half times denser than Aberdeen granite. Richard Atkinson used to tell in his lectures how re-erection of the stones blunted the country's best diamond-tipped drills. There is little the visitor can do to harm the stones, and he would have to outwit the guards.

The other part of the site is the ground. Having the public there, compacting this, it might be argued, was a positive advantage in that it helped hold the stones in place and lessen the actions of earthworms. These, Charles Darwin predicted, are quite capable of churning the soil until its structure is weakened and stones start to slip. He chose Stonehenge as his example. Don't they have worms at Stonehenge, or has Heseltine had them all banned? Another scientific problem is that all objects, like most humans, have a tendency to creep. It is all to do with the spin of the earth. There is also the long-term instability caused by chemical erosion of the chalk. Stonehenge is on the move in microscopic ways. Keeping the ground trampled firm has kept it more or less in its place for centuries.

The monument does not need saving from its public. Iain Nairn, writing in *The Sunday Times*, emphasised that the greatest virtue of Stonehenge was that it could be felt and touched. This physical thing, like stroking a cat or person who is special to one, is one of the root needs of humanity. Stonehenge is an experience. It is a point of contact with our past, its mysteries and its gods. Only bureaucrats and archaeologists could fail to see that.

Stonehenge has been manacled by our culture like mankind itself. It is appropriate, symptomatic of the growing repression and loss of freedom in every decaying civilisation on earth. Institutionalisation has to be mindless. It breeds further inanities. One appalling scheme of the 1970s was to surround the henge with a circular gallery, constructed like an Elizabethan theatre, so that the public could look down upon it from the walkways. Stonehenge would no longer have its nightly silhouette, against either the moon or the dirty yellow lights of Larkhill. You would drive past without seeing Stonehenge, only the outline of a football stadium concealing a game that had been cancelled. This crazy idea was announced from the Government benches in the House of Lords; one set of endangered species considering another.

Stonehenge has not had a good century. In 1920 *The Observer* railed at the prospect of shanty-town ribbon development along the road beside the monument. All the land was saved, hundreds of acres being placed in the ownership of the National Trust. Yet Stonehenge was still violated - some of its 1,438 acres of downland being rented out and ploughed into the same anonymity as the rest of the Wiltshire prairie. The Trust was to regard its Stonehenge estate as an agricultural asset, rather than a moment from the national dream. Land that was still regarded as sacrosanct and left grassed in the Iron Age and Roman periods is now pulled apart by the plough and dressed with agrochemicals. For all the problems of the Antrobus ownership the downs in private hands still ran sheep.

It might have been different if the ground had been acquired through Lord Eversley, as he had sound views on land management, and it was largely through his efforts (with the help of John Stuart Mill at Epping) that the London woods and heaths were preserved in the late nineteenth century. He had been quite prepared to launch a public appeal to buy Stonehenge for £10,000 - which, as he guessed, was actually above the market price for the monument. The owners rejected his £10,000 offer, but it was £6,600 that was bid at an auction in Salisbury in 1915. Cecil Chubb bought it because his wife had remarked over breakfast that "she would like to own it". They gave it to the nation in 1918 - which must have been among the nicer events of that year. Stonehenge had been saved, but it is no longer being shared.

Monuments, like works of art - and famous people - are always at risk. In the case of Stonehenge these are minimal, even in total, but it cannot be entirely free from them. An insurance evaluator would probably discount damage by visitors, but might think a more likely disaster would be an aircraft crash (there have been several in south Wiltshire) and particularly a publicity-seeking spectacular, like an attack upon the henge by a screwball pilot, or even on the ground from a drunken squaddy who's taken a tank. For Stonehenge, as for the rest of us, the chance of thermal nuclear war cannot be ruled out, and the monument suffers the disadvantage of sharing the vicinity with major military targets, including the aircraft research establishment at Boscombe Down and the country's principal artillery bases. These are risks that outweigh the dangers from human usage. If Stonehenge is to be rendered immune from just about everything then it will need to be covered with two hundred feet of earth.

In 1981 the Environment Department slightly relaxed its rule forbidding public access to the stones and, as an experiment, permitted visitors to walk among them on Tuesdays

Displaying Stonehenge

From Mr Jacob Simon

Sir, Bryan Kneale's letter (July 21) on the present condition of Stonehenge is especially timely, since the Department of the Environment is considering new proposals for the display of the monument and the reception of its well over half a million visitors a year. There is a danger, however, that this opportunity to ensure a more worthy setting for what is the most important prehistoric monument in Europe will be lost through a short-sighted approach.

The unsightly and inadequate nature of the existing reception facilities at Stonehenge led the last government to commission a special working party, including representatives from the department, the National Trust as owner, of the surrounding 1,400 acres of downland, and the local authorities. Their report in 1979, considering the long-term problems of the monument, was never published, but its recommendations received widespread support in this country and abroad.

However, opposition from local interests, in particular Salisbury District Council, led to the under secretary of state summarily rejecting its two most important findings, as was reported in your columns on August 29 last year. It was envisaged that all visitors facilities and car parking should be resited some distance away from the monument in Stonehenge Bottom, and that the A344 road, the nearer of the two roads passing right by the monument, should be closed and the traffic diverted a short distance along the A303. In this way, the stone circle could have been seen in the natural setting of the rich series of archaeological remains on the surrounding land and, most important, the once pervading sense of isolation at Stonehenge would have been repaired.

What then can now be done to alleviate the present sorry appearance of Stonehenge? Any proposal is going to cost money, as successive ministers have been quick to remark. The danger is that, rather than put the available funds towards what could be the first stage of a long-term solution, the department will opt for the easy but damaging approach of simply enlarging the existing facilities on the present site, so perpetuating past errors.

I believe that the nettle of relocating the present facilities and closing the road will have to be grasped if we are to achieve a solution of lasting value at Stonehenge. Whatever proposals there now are, need to be made available for public consultation as was promised by the department five years ago. Only in this way can an informed decision be reached on the future of Stonehenge.

Yours faithfully,
JACOB SIMON,
35 Courthope Road, NW3.

Jacob Simon's letter highlighted the continuing failure "to alleviate the present sorry appearance of Stonehenge"

Stonehenge setting

From the Director-General of The National Trust

Sir. Launching the National Trust's appeal for the purchase of some 1,400 acres of downland surrounding Stonehenge in 1927, the Prime Minister, Stanley Baldwin, wrote that "The solitude of Stonehenge should be restored, and precautions taken to ensure that our posterity will see it against the sky in the lonely majesty before which our ancestors have stood in awe throughout all our recorded history."

This cardinal principle has been and is still the Trust policy at Stonehenge. Compare the skyline today with photographs taken in the 1920s when a motley array of buildings competed with the monument. With support from the local community and the Office of Works, the worst of these unsightly intrusions were cleared away.

At Stonehenge today there are two threats whose effect could not have been fully anticipated in 1927. First is the great volume of traffic using the roads passing close to the monument. The A303 and A344 are physical and visual barriers cutting off the monument from the surrounding archaeological sites. Furthermore the noise of the traffic shatters the isolation and sense of awe that sensitive visitors seek at the monument. The A344 passes within feet of the Heel Stone and severs the monument from the Avenue approach.

This is why the Trust wholeheartedly supports Professor Atkinson (September 6) and Mr Underwood (August 31) in calling for the closure of the A344 where it passes beside the monument. The Trust has sympathy for those regular travellers among the local community whose journeys would be about one mile longer, but the pre-eminent importance of Stonehenge must be weighed against their inconvenience.

The second intrusion is the present car park and reception area, now manifestly inadequate for the half million visitors who come each year. The Trust welcomes the determination of the Department of the Environment in the long run to improve matters. As owner of the surrounding downs the Trust is willing to lease to the Department land for new services, provided the new site does not interfere with archaeological features and provided that its impact on the landscape is carefully considered. The cars and services must be out of sight from Stonehenge and also, so far as possible, from its main approaches.

The Trust participated in the working party and, as I have said, supports its recommendation to close the A344 and relocate the visitors' services. We advocate the publication of the report and the opportunity for wide public debate. The Department of the Environment has also told us of its wish to make short term improvements to the existing services on the present unsatisfactory site and we will support their proposals in so far as they do not prejudice the implementing of the fundamental changes described above.

Yours faithfully,
J. D. BOLES, Director-General,
The National Trust,
42 Queen Anne's Gate, SW1.
September 10.

from **THE TIMES TUESDAY SEPTEMBER 14 1982**

A

After David Loggan, who died in
1693, Loggan engraved two large
folding prints of Stonehenge, of
which this is a re-engraved French
reduction

Vûe de STONE-HENGE

Vûe de STONE-HENGE

I. Kip Sculp.

A The Stones call'd Cor
24 foot high, 7 broa
B The Stones call'd Car
C The place where

tones, 12 Tonn Weight
and 16 round
etts, of 6 or 7 Tonns
Mens bones are dug
up.

B

From Edmund Gibson's expanded
edition of William Camden's
'Britannia', 1695. The unknown
Dutch engraver, who worked from
a drawing, was told that there was
a castle on the hill behind the
monument – and engraved a
mediaeval fortress instead of the
banks of Vespasian's Camp

STONE

Number of the Stones 129, Height of the Largest Stones 20 Feet, Estimated W

Published by K

:NGE.

of Each 70 Tons, Diameter of the Circle formed by the Ditch 312 Feet.

rton, Sarum.

L

**From Walter Clapperton's mid-
nineteenth century 'Stonehenge
hand-book'**

John Constable's 'Stone Henge', 1845. The monument is seen from the south-east, from what is now the junction of the A 344 with the A 303 (the track to the left). The Heel Stone and the barrow beside Stonehenge are just beyond the cart on the other track

J.M.W. Turner's 'Stone Henge', from the 'Picturesque Views in England and Wales' published in 1829, featured the obligatory flock of the sheep around the monument — in the middle of a thunder storm with the shepherd struck dead by lightning and his dog howling at the moon.

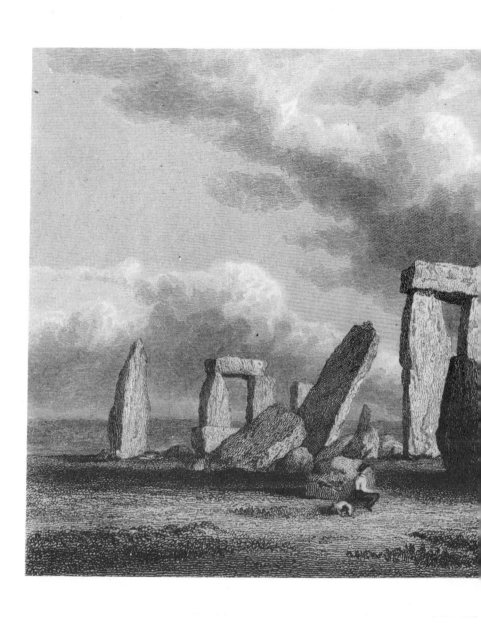

I

From William Westall's 'Great
Britain Illustrated', 1830

North East View of Stonehenge. From an Original Drawing

of George Keate Esq.r in the Possession of Rob.t Duke Esq.r

H. Roberts Sculp.

Sold by J. Easton Sarum.

H

From J. Easton's 'Conjectures on
Stonehenge', 1815

G

From the 'Tour and Residence in
Great Britain during the years 1810
and 1811 by a French traveller', L.
Simond.

F

**After Conrad Martin Metz, an
engraver born in Bonn in 1755, who
was living in London in 1808 and
died there some 25 years later**

A south View of STONE-HENGE, *on Sal*

ry plain, in the County of Wilts.

E

**From George Augustus Walpoole's
late eighteenth century 'Modern
British Traveller'**

D

From Francis Grose's 'Antiquities of England and Wales', published between 1773 and 1787

C

**By Edward Rooker, 1711-74,
engraved about 1750**